DRAMA

REMEDIAL DRAMA

A Handbook for Teachers and Therapists

Sue Jennings

Photos by George Solomonides

ADAM & CHARLES BLACK · LONDON
THEATRE ARTS BOOKS · NEW YORK

A & C Black (Publishers) Limited
35 Bedford Row, London WC1R 4JH

Reprinted 1982 (with revised appendices), 1984 (with revised appendices)

ISBN 0-7136-2232-6

Published simultaneously in the USA
by Theatre Arts Books, 153 Waverly Place, New York, NY 10014
ISBN 0-87830-563-7

Originally published in Great Britain 1973
by Pitman Publishing Limited
First published in paperback 1978

This book is dedicated to the memory of Ivor Mayne

Printed in Great Britain at the
University Press, Cambridge

Foreword

This book is a welcome reminder that therapy need not be treatment and need not be verbal.

Sue Jennings has developed her work with children and with adults who suffer from difficulties, either psychically or physically. She employs simple techniques and looks to understand each individual's communications other than, or in addition to, the purely verbal.

Language, which enabled Man to control his environment, to share himself and his information with others, also caused him sometimes to lose touch with himself (and at times caused him to lose touch with his significant others). Language in its distortions caused problems in communication.

Physical problems also cause disturbance in one's ability to communicate. There are many people, in any society, seeking to remedy problems and not knowing how to go about it. These problems are sometimes innate, sometimes secondary to malfunctioning, psychological and/or physical.

The therapeutic measures adopted, especially by medical and paramedical therapists, philosophers, clerics and others, have been largely verbal or explicable in verbal terms. They are understood cognitively, i.e. thinking arrives at comprehension.

For those working with children in the school setting there is a unique opportunity to begin to explore with an individual or group of children the dynamics of inner turmoil; to get in touch with it, and to share it. In this book this sort of experience is described and clearly thought-out techniques are suggested. The child or adult is given an experience, not conventional, but helpful as a beginning towards self-exploration and insight. It is an experience of physical discovery and relatedness — to his own body and to the peer group.

For teachers, a schema is gained of what is possible in coping with boisterous, hyperactive children, and also how to begin to make sense of processes which often appear inexplicable.

For those caring, for instance, for the withdrawn, ill or handicapped adult, there are other sorts of techniques described. Their purpose is to enable the individual to find, for himself, his own goodness, the worth of his own body and the ways in which he can express himself positively.

Therapy can never be available for all those who could benefit from it. Certainly the unique opportunity given to those who undergo psychoanalysis or psychiatric help is pathetically limited because of the paucity of therapists — and perhaps because society refuses to recognize its own illness.

More and more techniques aimed at getting in touch with children and those in trouble, techniques that are *enabling,* need to be developed.

This book is a welcome beginning. A helpful, chiefly technical survey of some of the methods which can be utilized in order to further self-fulfilment.

Tyrone Guthrie stated that the purpose of theatre is to show mankind to himself. The purpose of this book is to allow the individual — through the mediation of his teacher or therapist — to find himself for himself.

Dr Charles Enfield
Child Psychiatrist
Department of Children and Parents
Tavistock Clinic

Preface

This book has come about as a result of many requests from teachers and others for "things to do." It is intended for non-drama specialists such as teachers, social workers, occupational therapists, nurses and psychologists seeking new ideas to incorporate into their work. It will also provide stimulus for the trained drama leader to extend the scope of his work.

I hope that the book will emphasize just how much "drama" everyone already has in his own experience, though it is often known by other names such as "games." Although some ideas on drama training are included in this book, by far the most important factor in the work described is the basic attitude of the leader.

Obviously I have had to categorize and subdivide into sections, but these are arbitrary; many of the areas overlap and readers are advised to cross-refer. I have given as many practical ideas as possible of things to do rather than dwell on the philosophy behind them. All the suggestions have been tried out in remedial work but their success can only be gauged by the reader himself, trying them and seeing what happens.

If this book has a single message it must be that the *experience* of drama can enrich everyone's life whether mentally or physically handicapped, mentally ill or socially disadvantaged. There are no barriers to participation in drama.

Sue Jennings

Acknowledgements

I must thank the members of the Remedial Drama Group, especially Gordon Wiseman, and later the staff of the Remedial Drama Centre, who collectively pioneered more methods than I could have invented alone. Also the Rev. George Roe, Gerry Kershaw who shared many a thankless task with a smile, and the indefatigable Anne Bate. The children themselves — not least among them my own — were, of course, my best teachers.

Special mention must be made of my old student and friend Carole-Ann MacIntyre; and also Roy Shuttleworth, Alwyn Wareham, and Julia and George Solomonides, who have contributed to this book in so many ways.

I must thank the staff and patients of Anstalt Wittekindshof, especially Dr Alfred Sasse, and the pupils of St Luke's Special School, St Albans, and their former headmaster Mr P. Burt, for tolerance, understanding and enthusiasm.

My patron Harry Andrews, Dr Carlos Chan, Dr Patrick de Mare and then more recently Anthony Forge and Dr Salleh bin Sam, have had a profound influence on my thinking. A great source of inspiration too has been the work of Veronica Sherbourne, Dorothy Heathcote and Peter Slade.

Three people — Julia Johnson, Bob Morley and Tony Solomonides — have helped in ways that I am still discovering; these three I cannot thank enough.

And lastly, Sam Rughani has lived amongst the chaotic preoccupation with this book, and has always remained tranquil. To him, my very special thanks.

Sue Jennings

Contents

specialists — practical illustrations from an Approved
School — additional guidelines for psychotics — practical
illustrations from an autistic unit and a long-stay adult ward

1 What is Drama?

Since the aim of this book is primarily to provide a practical working handbook, I shall not be devoting lengthy chapters to the history and philosophy of drama; this has been ably done by many others and is under constant discussion and review by leading drama specialists. However, I must obviously offer an operational definition of this vague area known as drama.

In its widest sense drama can encompass all means of creative expression, with emphasis on the total participation of the group concerned and not on formal presentation to a static audience — "theatre." There is still confusion between the terms "theatre" and "drama" and in my frame of reference I regard theatre as being only a part of the whole field of dramatic expression.

I sometimes wonder if the label "drama" is not a disadvantage. As well as its theatrical connotations, its over-use in popular journalism for describing air crashes and coups associates the word "drama" with the unexpected, the crisis and often the disaster. Frequently I use other terms to counter possible anxiety or misunderstanding.

Drama is not a newly discovered activity. It has been an essential part of man's development from the earliest days, as is apparent from archaeological and anthropological research. In our own society it seems that creative expression has today become a minority activity. I think this is largely due to the effect of living in an age of "specialists." Instead of drama remaining part of our way of life, it has become, certainly in adult life, another choice of profession and one which frequently becomes polarized from the rest of society. Similarly, in many schools drama is set apart from other activities rather than inte-

1

grated into school policy as a whole. But drama is not merely an extra subject; it is a way of **doing**.

In preventive and therapeutic work we are largely concerned with improving communication and, in so doing, with assisting individuals and groups to build relationships. In contemporary society great value is placed on verbal communication — usually the person who attracts most attention is the one with most verbal dexterity. In individual and group psychotherapeutic disciplines also, verbal communication is all-important; where non-verbal approaches are used it is usually in order to develop verbal communication.

Yet language is a comparatively recent development in communication and forms only a small part of the range of drama, which incorporates all ways in which man can use himself to express his feelings through movement, dance, gesture, mime, sound or words. The baby and the young child have many ways of communicating without words and similarly, historically, man was able to communicate before he acquired words. Today, however, just as the growing child is discouraged from non-verbal communication, so modern man uses little except language. It may be an indication of man's insight in to his shortcomings that an increasing amount of his leisure time is being spent in the arts, or in encounter groups seeking "meaningful experiences."

As yet there has been little assessment of the wide variety of non-verbal approaches that can be used in preventive or therapeutic work and I would stress the great need for further exploration in this direction.

I would suggest that in order to communicate satisfactorily the individual must feel free to express himself (i.e. his own individuality) and that from this communication comes the groundwork for relationship-building. Furthermore, the **group** must be able to express their group feelings and reinforce the group identity. Non-verbal communication is very necessary for expressing those feelings which do not need words (or for which there are no words); in fact for expressing the pre-verbal side of man. It can also provide an alternative means of communication for the person who cannot or will not speak. For some, words have become too dangerous, too committing. One of my young clients, who had opted out of speaking although otherwise developing quite normally, was found to come from a home where words were only used between the parents for battles of a most vicious nature. Neither parent spoke to the child and it was scarcely surprising that he was not prepared to risk such a destructive means of communication. Gradually, with sympathetic creative play therapy, his confidence was restored and development became possible.

The creativity and imagination of the young child are usually referred to as "play." Psychologists and educationalists alike have long realized the importance of play for the developing child. The child who is prevented from play will be impoverished mentally, emotionally and physically. A boy referred to me as severely subnormal was prevented from playing at home: he was restricted to a spotless white hallway, with balloons and a teddy-bear for his only toys. He was not allowed to feed himself and was force-fed on liquids. When the child was later abandoned and taken into a foster home with plenty of play stimulus, his development was found to be normal.

Much of children's play consists of taking on roles and playing out life situations to be encountered later. Erikson[1] wrote that play is the microcosm of the macrocosm; that all its dramatic actions in little are the big actions of real life. This is already made use of in play school activities such as the Wendy House, and also in more specialized forms of play therapy at child-guidance clinics. But need it stop there? I would suggest that there is a need for play in all of us — hence the well-known anecdotes of adults giving children toys with which they themselves would like to play — but the older we get the fewer the opportunities we have to play. Instead, the urge to play is channelled elsewhere. Many years ago one of my lecturers suggested, to the astonishment of his students, that politics was just a grown-up way of playing games. Play is too often regarded in our society as childish and therefore unacceptable. True, it is child-like but surely it should not be forbidden to the adult. I have often thought that adventure playgrounds for tired business men would relieve much social tension. Certainly, play is an important element in remedial drama work with all ages.

There is a tendency among educationalists and drama leaders

[1] In his book *Childhood and Society* (Penguin).

to emphasize the use of drama for exploring and experiencing new feelings, dimensions and ideas. It is my belief that the ritual part of drama, the expression of the known, the familiar and the "safe" is equally important. Ritual is often thought to be synonymous with bongo drums and bare feet, but it is much more than this. Consider the many group rituals which give different groups their identity — from the Zulu war dance to Girl Guide campfire songs, from a Welsh eisteddfod to playground skipping songs. Only when adherence to ritual becomes anti-social — the bovver boy cult, for example — obsessional or repetitive, as with the recidivist or the autistic's compulsive rocking, should we seek ways of altering existing patterns and establishing new ones. In these last examples the ritual has become negative and destructive whereas it should be a positive statement of social identity, a safe base from which other activities can be developed. Drama can thus be considered as a means of reinforcing the known as well as finding out about the unknown. It is ritual which gives a group its identity and which can also provide a framework for the discovery of new identities.

Nobody questions the assumption that drama is relevant to the developing child, who will cope satisfactorily with new challenges only if he has been able to express and understand his inner feelings and conflicts. If we accept this need in the normal growing child, how much more important is it for the child whose paths of communication has been warped or severely damaged?

In order to correct mistaken impressions, I must emphasize that remedial drama does not itself differ in content or technique from other types of drama, although great care must be taken in selecting and applying drama techniques to remedial work. Once you are confident in using these techniques, there is little to worry about — in spite of the fears of one headmistress, who refused to allow drama at all in her school because, she said, it was dangerous. When pressed to explain her views, she said, "Start something like that and they'll all become so primitive. You never know what might happen" — as if drama were some kind of Pandora's Box that might let loose all sorts of chaos! It is interesting to note, too, that our worried headmistress equates "primitive" behaviour with total permissiveness of the "orgies in the jungle" type. Even a cursory look at truly "primitive" expression will show that it is *so* ritualized, *so* group-oriented, that it leaves no scope for individual expression, let alone unboundaried indulgence.

ATTITUDES OF THE LEADER
Is there an ideal drama leader? I would suggest that there is, but emphasize that in work of the kind described here it is the **attitude** of the leader rather than any formal dramatic training which defines this ideal.

Teachers often say to me that to do drama would be "super" and then, "but of course I don't have the training" as if assuming that the subject-matter learnt, the voice production and the movement, is the crucial factor. If drama could be seen more simply as a way of doing something, a flexible framework in which things can happen, perhaps more people would realize that they already have the experience of their own childhood on which to draw. Playground games, stories and action songs are just a part of the rich heritage which can help us in a drama session. If we look back for a moment again, we can probably re-call times when, after a terrifying nightmare, it would have help-ed if we could have "played it out" instead of being told to forget all about it; or times when we could have gained confid-ence and reassurance before going to a new school or into hospital if we could have anticipated the experience by improv-ising it in a drama session. The ability to recall "how we felt" on such occasions will help to provide the empathy, the sense of mutual communication, needed in a drama session. Such sessions, too, can be far more effective as demonstrations of "the other side of the story" than possibly meaningless moral sanctions.

The most difficult task facing the leader is to strike a balance between working freely within a structure which is flexible but secure, and doing drama to a rigid formula. The temptation to create structures is great — it is not easy to stimulate ideas from the group without superimposing personal opinions as to how a situation should develop. How often do we think of a marvellous idea for a project or improvisation and throw out the stimuli, hoping the group will pick up the wave-length and respond in the way we would choose? A session is more rewarding, however, when we are able to provide the

stimulus and then step back in order to encourage and develop
what spontaneously occurs.

Of course many people fear that the only alternative to formal
structure is an aimless, self-indulgent meandering, lacking any
control. But if a leader has enough confidence to provide and
support the secure framework, and enough patience to wait
and see, positive imaginative activity will be encouraged. The
leader has to be able to become involved in a situation, to be
part of it, without losing his overall awareness of the group. If
we consider him as being involved eighty per cent, then the
remaining twenty per cent remains detached and provides the
framework.

An awareness of mood in the group, and an ability to respond
to its changes, are a great advantage to a leader. A session will get
off to a good start if the leader can sense the mood of the group
when he first meets them. He should then be able to tune in to
the changing needs of the group so that he knows for example
when there has been enough stimulation and a slackening of pace
is needed; this must be done smoothly, within the context of the
session and without disrupting the ongoing activity. Or a personal
situation may evolve from a group activity; if the leader is aware
of such a change he can decide to contain or to explore the
situation, whichever is appropriate.

I have been told more than once that "Teachers should not be
therapists." This depends on how we define the role of the
therapist; whilst teachers are obviously not equipped to replace
the psychotherapist it cannot be denied that there are overlaps
in the responsibility of all professions concerned with the overall
mental, physical and emotional well-being of the population.
Furthermore there are skills and techniques in specialized fields,
such as group dynamics and role playing, which can be used by
all "caring" disciplines.

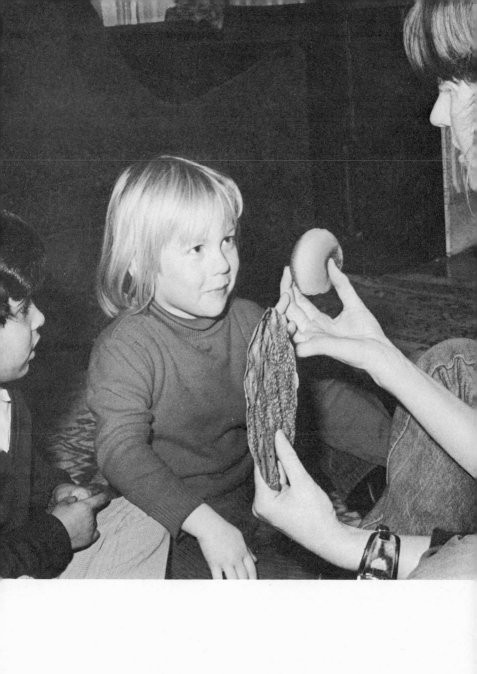

2 Practical Suggestions

In this chapter we shall be looking at the drama resources available to a group leader and how they can be used. It is very daunting for the non-expert to be faced with a barrage of mystical expressions such as dance drama or improvisation; add adjectives like on-going or experiential and the leader may feel that he has become involved in some extraordinary cult. I will therefore keep technical terms to a minimum.

The following are dramatic components but should not be considered as isolated categories. They can be used in innumerable combinations.

Movement, Dance and Mime are important means of physical expression which in Western society tend to be channelled into very structured forms such as sport and various formal dance techniques, for instance ballet for little girls. There is an unfortunate tendency for movement to become a specialist area in itself when it could be linked with the drama field as a whole.

At its simplest, body expression (like visual art and music) provides a way of communicating non-verbally which can complement society's emphasis on verbal communication. Physical contact — a reassuring hand on the shoulder, for example — can communicate a direct supportive statement where words would be inappropriate.

It is essential for a child to be aware of his own body — the whole and the individual parts — and its potential. From this he will build up body identity and awareness and will learn to understand his strength. Through movement the child can be helped to develop his body as a means of communication and the adult can be reminded of its potential.

Possibly as a result of living in a "machine age," many .

people are forgetting how to use their bodies and become tense and unco-ordinated; the purpose of tension, to avert accidents or to cope with crises, has become distorted by the strain of living with excess noise and overcrowding. Today, relaxation is something that frequently has to be **learnt.**

Improvisation can be movement or dance or words, sounds or silence and in response to a variety of visual, auditory or tactual stimuli. Its essence is the spontaneity of something happening here and now. If the experience is repeated (and many people love to repeat enjoyable discoveries) then it is no longer improvisation, although it is still valuable and can form part of a ritual from which in turn new things are improvised.

Project Work often grows from improvisation; in it specific themes are developed usually supported by background work and linked to other media. It can create an ideal learning situation but should always leave room for fantasy as well as fact.

Masks and Make-up and other aids all broaden the scope and dimensions of drama; they are discussed in Chapter 11, "Further Practical Suggestions."

Other Creative Media must at least be mentioned. It is impossible to separate drama from art and music, even though the tendency of our schools and colleges is to provide training in a specific category. Moods very often need to be expressed through paint and sound as well as through words and movement. The creative media should be seen as complementary and interdependent, rather than isolated one from the other.

The rest of this chapter will be devoted to simple ideas which can be adapted to a wide variety of age and ability. They can be used as a starting point and could be especially useful to those new to the field of drama. Remember that all that is needed to "do drama" is a group of people and a space.

STARTING THE SESSION

A class will pick up the leader's feelings very quickly if he or she is anxious or ambivalent, so an atmosphere of confidence tinged with a drop of anticipation will help to establish security.

When trying drama for the first time, a ten-minute session

slotted into, and forming a natural part of, a class is usually a good "try-out" and enables the leader to gain confidence. A general knowledge or current-affairs lesson could end with a re-enactment of an item or story which particularly interested the class.

Simple routine actions, like lining-up for assembly, can be dramatized: "See if you can line up as though you are burglars, stealthily leaving a house"; "Sit in your chairs as if you are made of wood/clay/metal" (or a very old lady/a young baby/waiting for some good news/bad news). Starts of this nature often produce far more absorption than an announcement, "We're going to do drama now" — the latter always conjures up pre-conceptions of what they are about to do.

Any part of the school timetable can incorporate the kind of approach described above and the leader will find it less daunting than initially having to face a whole session of drama. A small beginning can slowly be lengthened as the group and the leader gain confidence.

As the session expands, thought must be given to the size of the group, since pressure of numbers often decides the nature of the activity. Frequently there is no choice in the matter — it is either the whole class or not at all. When I have been in a position to dictate numbers I find an ideal average is ten members, less with the severely handicapped and more if I have assistants. Some children and adults cannot cope immediately with participating in large group activity and in these cases I have found it necessary to work individually or in very small groups initially before progressing to larger group work. Think carefully when assigning your groups —it can be mortifying to say "all get into pairs" and find there is one child left over. If there is an odd number, you could suggest "get into twos and threes" or "would someone like to be my partner?".

CREATING ENVIRONMENTS

First the group must get to know its working area. If the room is familiar they may well huddle together and wait for direction. This often occurs when they are feeling apprehensive about what is going to happen, and can be avoided if there is some-thing new for them to find — posters on the wall, a particular piece of music that creates a mood, or a suggestion from the leader to discover the room in a new way: "How long a journey can you make without touching the floor?", "Can you travel from one end to the other on your back?", "Look at the room backwards through your legs."

Teachers are often harassed when their class scatters and appears out of control. To explore an unfamiliar room is very natural, however, and gives the group a chance to know and feel at home in their surroundings (most people do this in new situations, such as in a hotel room or a new house). Ideally, this can be built into the beginning of the session. Remember that "a space for activity" is all that is needed. There is no need for a fully equipped studio. (See Chapter 11 regarding equipment suggestions.)

SUGGESTIONS

"Explore the room and see how many different sounds you can find..." these sounds may be used to tell stories, hold conversations (we had a beautiful conversation for ten minutes between a doorknob and a radiator) or for orchestration: after the sounds have been explored an orchestra can be composed of radiators, floor, chairs, waste-paper bins and coat-hangers, with the leader conducting initially and later anyone who wants a turn. Each member of the group can play individually and then together in a variety of speeds and rhythms. (A teacher once asked me in desperation what I would do with a child who only rubbed pipes and blew raspberries. My answer was "Orchestrate the raspberries!")

"Explore the room on your hands and feet . . . . what does it feel like?. . . what noises does it make? . . . explore it with all of you, even your nose and your hair . . . ." (The questions are not to provoke a verbal answer but to stimulate a physical response.)

If the group settles into this activity, suggest that they close their eyes and continue exploring; it can produce a remarkably high degree of involvement and absorption. If it also produces giggles when the children touch each other or end up in a knot on the floor — why not?

If a drama room is multi-purpose, it is often not possible to have adventurous equipment. Imagination must therefore be used to let chairs become barricades, space ships or factory machinery. A budget is nice but not essential. Indeed, over-sophisticated

equipment and too much stimulus in the environment can blunt
creativity rather than develop it. Some of the most successful
sessions have been those where children were able to create their
own surroundings rather than come into them ready made.

EXTENDING THE ENVIRONMENT

One fairly easy way to alter even a familiar environment is by
varying the lighting.

If it is possible to black out windows, simple effects may
be created by hanging brightly coloured material over "cold"
fluorescent lights; using coloured light-bulbs; or using a single
light, leaving the rest of the space in shadow and darkness
(withdrawn children in particular respond to a dimly lit room,
feeling perhaps that they cannot be seen). Some school halls do
have basic lighting equipment and individual spotlights with
colour filters can be used to create atmosphere.

In many modern buildings there is too much glass to facilitate adventurous lighting, so greater emphasis must be placed
on changing the shape and contours of the room. Portable
rostra are invaluable; and so are inexhaustible supplies of large
cardboard boxes, large pieces of sheeting and curtaining as well
as string, ribbon and lengths of computer paper. We once had
a room full of cobwebs made from string and torn-up sheeting
and the group derived as much benefit from the co-operation
necessary to change the room as they did from improvising with
it afterwards. This same cobweb environment, together with a
simple piece of electronic music, provided the basis for an
underwater improvisation.

If it is necessary to have a tidy room at the end of the session,
try and build it into the activity instead of making it a boring
chore afterwards. One of my staff formed the cleaners' army,
wearing tin helmets and complete with a sergeant inspecting
the mops and brushes!

SUGGESTIONS

Leave the room bare apart from a large heap of cardboard
boxes. Make sure there is a large box for each member of the
group. "Use a box as anything to travel in." Allow several
minutes for this as children change their ideas and think out

new ones. "Carry your box as if it is very very precious and breakable." This can be continued as an imaginative game using the boxes for all different types of functions, but take care to stop before the group gets bored.

Suggest the group get into twos and threes: "You are furniture removers. You've got to carry this large and very heavy furniture down a steep narrow staircase." All sorts of situations may develop out of this and lead into improvised scenes. The leader can gauge from the absorption of the group how long this should continue. If it is necessary to move on to a new topic, the numbers could be varied: divide the class in half and suggest that one group have got to use all their boxes for inventing a machine for transporting provisions and equipment up a mountain and that the other group invent a trap for capturing the abominable snowman/ elephants/the magic hoola bird that lives in the mountain. Permutations on this simple theme are endless both for individual and large group work.

SOUND
Sound and particularly music can be used to create environments — but the group must be quiet enough to hear what is being played! It is no good trying to use sound to combat the noise already going on — the group will only shout louder! (See Chapter 9.) If the children are sitting or lying on the floor with their eyes closed and the sound is slowly brought up to volume on the record player, this attentiveness will increase their involvement. Detailed suggestions for appropriate music can be found in Chapter 11; always beware of using a sound stimulus that is too vague. Let the group explore their own reactions to a piece even though you may feel its mood is obvious!

SUGGESTIONS
Choice of music: "The Ride of the Valkyries." "You are all asleep on the deck of a large ocean liner. Some of you are passengers going on a luxury cruise, some of you are members of the crew. As you lie down to sunbathe in this very hot tropical sun, decide for yourselves who you are and what you do, what you would be wearing." (Allow time for settling down and quietness.) "Everything is very peaceful and there is

scarcely any movement in the boat, and then you hear . . . ."
(slowly bring up music). Further comment from the leader may
not be necessary and this is the type of situation that has to be
played purely by ear and allowed to go on to its natural
conclusion.

MOVEMENT
From my own experience if a class is labelled as "movement"
or "dance" the group often arrives with preconceived ideas,
usually negative ones, about what they will be asked to do
(dancing is "something cissy that girls do"); but under the
general heading "drama" the toughest boys are likely to participate is scaling mountains, hacking their way through the
jungle or combating the elements. All of these exercises require
a high degree of physical skill and co-ordination.

   Although many drama sessions will include body movement
as well as other forms of expression there are exercises concentrating on the physical aspect which can be developed on their

own. This provides opportunities for extending body development and co-ordination outside the range of everyday movement. (In many schools there will be a problem of space for
doing movement; this type of difficulty is discussed more fully
in Chapter 11.)

It is necessary both to relax the body and to "warm it up,"
rather like an athlete toning up his muscles. Although it is
advantageous to start with relaxation to gain the group's
concentration, it is scarcely appropriate to attempt something
so tame with a crowd of lusty nine-year-olds tearing round the
hall making Tarzan cries. In these instances it is better to
commence with a far more vigorous physical activity!

Remember that one of the symptoms of many of those in
remedial groups is inability to relax; relaxation frequently has
to be taught. Young children are unable to respond to abstract
descriptions — it is no use saying "Now I want you all to relax."
However, it is quite simple to achieve relaxation through
imaginative exercises; cats, both domestic and jungle, are an
ideal example of complete relaxation.

SUGGESTIONS

'What does it feel like to be a cat curled up in front of a very
warm fire asleep. . . fast asleep and the fire feels very warm. . .
feel the heat warming you. . . slowly you start dreaming of milk,
and then maybe you start to wake up, stretch one paw at a
time, until you stretch right the way through. . . stretch . . .
but you curl up and go to sleep again in the warm. . ." Continue
into waking, drinking milk: "What does a cat do after drinking
milk? He might wash his face," etc. New gestures are brought
in: hunting a mouse, sharpening claws, stalking, pouncing,
playing, ending up with going back to sleep.

Examples of lions, tigers, squirrels hibernating after picking
nuts, or human examples of being in bed and waking up in
the morning, can be used. There are many ideas involving
sleep and warmth, waking up and going back to sleep, which
will all encourage relaxation.

Older groups may feel too sophisticated to "go to sleep"
or play at animals. The leader can still make use of ideas
involving tension and its release: "We are all going to blow
up a balloon. It can be any size, shape or colour you like."

Slowly blow up the balloons; very good for breathing. Then:
"Tie the top (incorporating intricate movement), find a pin
(usually out of hair, off floor or in lapel) and 1. . . 2. . . 3. . .
BANG!" After two or three times the sequence of the exercise
will be established. Let the group divide into pairs to blow each
other up as balloons (expanding from curled, crouch position
on floor until standing up fat and tall) and prick one another
with an imaginary pin. Gradually the group will achieve the
physical contrast between the tension of being blown up and
the slow letting out of air until the "balloon" is crumpled and
relaxed on the floor. Everyone can have a turn at being a balloon
and a blower. This exercise could always lead into group
balloons with half the group, arms round shoulders in a circle,
being the balloon and the other half outside the circle blowing
vigorously.

Although the main purpose of the balloon exercise is relaxation, it also stimulates the imagination and enables the body to
BE different things; it also encourages co-operation in pairs and
groups.[1]

Weight-lifting is another favourite with older children; trying
to lift weights, succeeding, and then putting them down provides
a useful tension-release sequence.

The above exercises must have the backing of the leader's
voice, alternately relaxed and tense. Remember that the group
will be influenced by the tone of your voice and also your
movement.

It is not always possible to use imaginative description, for
instance with severely subnormal groups. However, the feeling
of relaxation can be achieved through gentle movement to
appropriate music. (BUT still use verbal backing to the music
and movement when possible.) Example: with the group in a
circle holding hands, start with slow swaying of the body from
side to side (the group could be sitting on the floor, on chairs
or standing up). The feel of rocking or "waves" can slowly
encompass the whole body through to hands, arms, head. It
can be done with the whole group or in small groups or pairs.

[1] I describe this exercise in some detail because it has been a well-tried favourite
over the last ten years in many schools and hospitals throughout Europe; during
second visits children and adults would always ask first for "der Luftballon" or
"le ballon."

Whatever the encouragement some children will remain tense for a very long time and their movement will tend to be small and inhibited. It is possible to help the body to be opened, extended and the tension released. With those who allow physical contact I have found the most effective way of facilitating relaxation is to transmit it through my own body: if the child is sitting on the floor and I am standing behind him (having of course got to know him face to face first, or this would be alarming) I place my feet on either side of his buttocks, my knees against the back and my hands on the shoulders with his hands in mine. There are then four points of body contact and I do the swaying exercises with the child.

Adults, although more able to respond to the abstract idea of relaxation, also enjoy imaginative exercises. Situations such as a favourite place to go on holiday and soak up the sun or responding to tranquil music facilitate relaxation even in the chronically tense.

Having got the group as relaxed as possible, we can introduce more stimulated movement, designed to exercise and develop. "Warming up" is used to tone up the whole body and encourage awareness of its many parts. Warm-ups should be fun, often laughed at (laughter tones up the system and releases tension), and the music should be light and rhythmic, with very careful gauging of speed (see Chapter 11). Rhythm on a tambour can also be used and in time the group will develop their own body rhythms.

"Jokey-jerky-jump-about." Start with shaking hands vigorously together and alternately. Add alternate feet, the whole arm, legs, hips, head until the whole body is shaking; stand still, set up a shake that goes right through the whole body, not forgetting knees and shoulders. Many children can do this but keep their face muscles quite static. Pause for a moment and let the group explore with their hands to see just how flexible their face muscles are, pulling funny faces, etc. Then without using hands shake all the face muscles. Repeat the whole exercise.

Simple running, walking, jumping, leaping sequences all make good warm-ups. Make sure there is plenty of variety and contrast of speed, rhythm and texture. Encourage the group to be

adventurous ("let's try boxing with our elbows"); let different
body parts have conversations with each other (by means of
movement, not words), fingers "talking" to toes, shoulders to
ears; suggest each child finds a partner — two pairs of knees
meeting and greeting. This is preferable to making a definitive
statement such as, "Move like a giraffe," which gives a whole
body identity before the potential of individual body parts has
been developed.

Always include small, fine movement —picking up very small
objects like birds' eggs, marbles or pins, with fingers and toes.

As well as stimulating separate body parts contrast this with
using the whole body: (Music should not be necessary for these.)
"Make yourself as small as you can. . . as large as you can. . . as
flat as you can so that you can crawl under a door. . . ." "With
your partner find as many ways as you can of going over, under
or through your partner" — can be done in twos or threes
and encourages imagination and co-operation.

It is important for girls and boys to be able to test their own
physical strength and a simple exercise in pairs, hands on each
other's shoulders trying to push each other across the room
is a very good starter. There are many variations — holding
hands and pulling each other, taking it in turns to roll their
partner from one end of the room to the other with their partner
either completely floppy or very rigid.

Many of the exercises already described could be classified as
"mime," and of course these can be developed in their own right
to help clarity, co-ordination and inventiveness. Rather than say
to a class "We're not going to talk" it is better to suggest "Let's
talk with our hands/face/bodies," or "I wonder what it was like
before we invented words."

I use little pre-choreographed dance with remedial groups
compared with the proportion of creative movement. I find
groups of most ages enjoy composing their own dances to, for
example, reggae music. Often, the leader can start off the
dance and then let each member of the group continue the
sequence. The group will enjoy having created something of their
very own and this of course helps to reinforce the group identity.
There is a great deal of scope, too, in the use of cross-cultural
dance and music, which will be dealt with more fully in
Chapter 3, "Drama with Immigrants."

WORDS AND SOUNDS
Many individuals take a long time before they are prepared to
improvise speech alone in a group situation. However, prepare
for vocal work, using the relaxation — warm-up principles that
have already been described for movement. There is a large
range of vocal work that can be done to develop confidence for
speech — sound effects, group singing, discovering the range of
noise the voice can make. Perhaps the best time to begin
verbal improvisation is when the group have got to know each
other and the leader and have tried vocal work in unison.

SUGGESTIONS
Tell the group a story which involves a lot of noisy effects
contrasted with light delicate sounds. The story could be
about a journey, for instance, encountering different hazards
such as thunder-storms or earthquakes, with the rain becoming
quieter and quieter until it is nothing, or the earthquake noises
sounding farther and farther away.

The leader can judge how much to assist or participate;
it can be reassuring to use a drum or tambour to encourage
and accompany the group's vocal sounds.

The leader can start off a session on sound with everyone
sitting down and "If I were in a hospital/factory/zoo what
noises would I hear?" Try a story about a ghost house with
the group making the eerie creaks and groans. In time this
could be developed into an improvisation: you could divide
the class in half and let one half make the ghost sounds while
the other half explores the haunted house.

A group's first try-out at verbalization can be around favourite topics taken from television and films such as "Tarzan,"
"Frankenstein," "Z Cars" or even a television commercial.
This is fine, because it is an area that they know and understand
and enjoy re-creating. Always be ready to move on from the
familiar and gently introduce a new element.

"I wonder what would happen if Tarzan and Frankenstein
met in the jungle," or "Suppose James Bond is appointed the
new Chief of New Town Police Station."

Many groups will want to re-create situations that they have
personally experienced, such as a court appearance, or a big

bust-up at home. Individuals can obtain relief and insight through this, as can the rest of the group by empathy and identification. I prefer these situations to arise spontaneously and this does happen when a particular theme reminds somebody of his own experience.

We have just been improvising a courtroom scene and a thirteen-year-old boy comes up and says, "I've been in court." He begins to elaborate. Leader: "Don't tell me about it, show me. Who else was there?" It is best to let the child choose the characters himself from other members of the group. He may want to play himself, his Dad in an angry scene or perhaps the magistrate. Allow him this freedom. From time to time you can suggest "role reversals," i.e. the playing of different characters, in order for him to gain insight and understanding and also a chance to vent his feelings about the people concerned (see Chapter 10).

The range of verbal situations that could be improvised and developed is vast and enriching. After the early stages the group will find it easier to contribute their own ideas, probably diverse, original and colourful. Be scrupulously fair about letting as many people pool material as possible and not all shouting at once!

STORIES
Stories are usually envisaged as a passive activity where the group either sit quietly while a story is read, or read quietly to themselves. However, stories provide a natural framework for drama activity. After all, they have a beginning, a middle and an end.

The range of themes is vast and can encompass well-loved fairy and adventure stories or ones newly created by the leader or group. Familiar stories have an advantage because they are known and provide a safe ritual beginning. Imagination can be stretched by putting the familiar story into a new context: "What would happen if Jesus was born this year?" Books on myth and legend supply rich sources for new story lines.

There are various ways or organizing a story session. The leader can tell the story as the action unfolds (see the Oseo story below); a new story can be improvised while it is going

on — "And what happened next?"; alternatively it can be improvised without any narration at all. We have already mentioned other uses of stories under "Words and Sounds."

In handling a dramatized story session, particularly with young groups, it is better for everybody to play everybody in the story than to cast individual parts; it is rather unfair for individual children to be Red Riding Hood, the Wolf and Grandma while the others, feeling hard done by, have to be the trees in the wood.

SUGGESTIONS

THE STORY OF OSEO (adapted from a North-American Indian legend). Start with the group cross-legged on the floor, suggesting that they are sitting in wigwams, and give an introductory chat about everyday life of the Indians — what did they wear? what did they eat for breakfast. . .?

"Oseo was an Indian boy who lived in a village very near the forest. He was always getting into scrapes and had far more adventures than all the other children.

"One day he was sitting in his wigwam carving a piece of wood with his sheath knife (action starts) and wondering how to stop being bored. He decided to go and explore a new forest path so he jumped up, put on his jacket with the secret pockets, his special shoes which are called. . ., and crept quickly and quietly out of his tent, over the fence and into the dark forest.

"Although mischievous, Oseo always remembered the forest code, that whenever he heard a noise he must stop, look and listen because it could be something dangerous. He went on down the path whistling to himself, wondering where it would lead, and suddenly he heard a loud screech. So he. . . (wait for class to respond with action or words) yes, he stopped, looked and listened. . . But it was only the magic hoola bird flying away in the treetops so Oseo went on his way.

"The path got narrower and narrower and creepers began to get in his way. Soon he was pushing through the under-growth, over fallen logs. . . clambering over boulders. . . and hacking his way through shrubs and bushes with his pocket knife. He came to a clearing and sat down for a rest under a large tree. He noticed a tiny bird at the foot of the tree and looked up and saw it must have fallen out of its nest. He gently picked it up, stretched on tiptoe and just managed to put it back. He was just going when the mother bird came to the edge of the nest and said 'Don't go Oseo, I've got a surprise for you. You've been very kind to me.' Oseo stretched up his hand wondering what it could be and was a little disap-pointed when the bird put a small dried pea into his palm, but she said, 'Take good care of this because it's magic.' So Oseo put it in his secret pocket and went on his way.

"He followed the path again and had to jump across several ditches. Suddenly he heard a strange whirring sound, so he. . . stopped, looked and listened, but it was only a rattlesnake which slid away into the undergrowth and did not trouble him. He came to the banks of a river and was wondering how to get across when he saw a squirrel sitting by the water crying. Oseo asked him what the matter was and the squirrel said that he wanted to cross the river but couldn't swim. Oseo said, 'That's all right, you can sit on my head and I

will take you across.' He carefully lifted the squirrel, placed
him on his head and began to wade into the water. It was
very cold and came up to his ankles, then his knees, then his
tummy, then his feet couldn't feel the bottom and he began
to swim to the other side. He stepped out of the water and
put the squirrel down. He squeezed his clothes dry and jumped
up and down to get warm again. Meanwhile the squirrel had
disappeared and then came back and said, 'You've been
very good to me Oseo, I want to give you a present.' Oseo
held out his hand and the squirrel gave him an acorn.He was
very disappointed but the squirrel said, 'It's magic, Oseo,
keep it with you and it might help you one day.' Oseo said
goodbye, climbed up a grassy bank and over a fence into a
large field.

"He was running around in the grass feeling very happy and
suddenly heard 'Ehhhhhaahhhhhhhhh.' He stopped, looked
and listened and saw the most enormous giant coming towards
him, 'Ehhhhhaahhhhhhhhh.' Oseo began to run but the giant
was getting nearer and bellowed 'I'm going to catch you,
Oseo, for my dinner tonight' and he threw a huge net over
him. Oseo struggled and struggled but the net got tighter and
tighter and more and more tangled and he couldn't move
at all. The giant stomped off saying he was going to fetch a
cooking pot. Oseo felt very sad and knew he would never
see his village again and started to cry. Then he remembered
the bird's present — he managed to get one hand free to get
the magic pea out of his secret pocket. He put it on the end
of his tongue, closed his eyes and wished very very hard, and
sure enough he began to get smaller, and smaller, until he
was so small that he was able to climb out through one of
the holes in the net. He began to run towards the river and heard
the giant coming in the background. All the grass felt like an
enormous forest and was prickling his legs and scratching him.
Tiny pebbles seemed like great big rocks. He got to the fence
and lay on his tummy and wriggled underneath, rolled down
the bank and stood by the river realizing he was too small to
get across. The giant was getting nearer — what could he do?
Yes. . . the acorn. He got it out of his secret pocket, put it
on the end of his tongue, closed his eyes and wished very hard.
Sure enough he began to grow bigger and bigger until he was

back to his normal size again. He dashed into the river, swam
as fast as he could to the other side, didn't wait to dry himself
and started running along the path. He came to the clearing,
sprinted across it and then came to the hard bit where he had
to fight his way through the undergrowth. Everything got in
his way but at last he got through and there was the path
again leading to the camp. He got to the fence and very quietly
climbed over, went to his wigwam and gave a sigh of relief.
He took off his Indian jacket, put his moccasins by the door
and sat down cross-legged on the floor. He began whittling his
piece of wood again and thinking about his big adventure;
but when anyone came past his tent they would never have
thought anything had happened."

Besides being a very popular story Oseo's adventure can
be an all-embracing drama session — it includes several shades
of feeling, happiness, sadness, caring, fear; a large range of
movement for combating the forest; it has a built-in control
factor: "Stop, look and listen"; and it provides concentration,
stimulation and ample opportunity for "calming down"
at the end.

NATIVITY THEME

The class had discussed what it would be like if Jesus were
born now, and had come up with various ideas: one said "Of
course Mary would be an unmarried mother, wouldn't she?"
and "She'd have to get help from the Welfare." We developed
some of the aspects in improvisation (such as interviews with
Social Security) and put them together in story form.

The story opened with Mary and Joseph wandering suburban
streets, homeless and without money. Eventually they rested
in a bus shelter where Mary had her baby with an anxious
Joseph dialling 999 to summon an ambulance. Policemen
arrived to move them on and a crowd gathered through which
ITV and BBC camera crews fought their way to get live
coverage. The local councillors came to register protests at
this unseemly behaviour but then realized that with TV
coverage they would stand to gain by helping the couple. So
the housing officer promised to find them a council house as
soon as Mary came out of hospital where the ambulance had

rushed her. The crowd made speeches and debated the issue as to whether it was fair for somebody with only one child to jump the housing queue. One of the children summed up the matter by saying, "Well it's different, innit? 'E's special."

I tried the same theme in a psychiatric clinic when it was suggested that we should be getting Christmassy. The patients decided that Mary would be a coloured immigrant trying to get access into Britain to have her baby on the National Health Service. They dramatized her difficulties at the airport, resolved them by her getting a forged passport and finished up with the couple wandering around Piccadilly Circus. Various characters such as social workers were brought in and presented as being ineffectual and unable to help. Eventually the couple found themselves squatting and were visited by three wise men — a Tory, a Socialist and an anti-immigrant politician. The first two waxed poetic on the help they would give at some unspecified date in the future; the last presented Mary with a pair of scissors to decapitate her children saying, "It'll be easier in the long run, won't it dear?" Mary, incidentally, had given birth to three children. The story ended with the squatters fleeing the house to go to Buckingham Palace hoping to find sympathy there, but already feeling that they would be permanently on the run.

This well-known story, the birth of Jesus, provided an ideal framework for a lot of "socially unacceptable" feelings to be expressed through the patients playing other roles. They obtained release by feeling free to portray Government officials, social workers, etc., and were able to gain insight into their own behaviour.

3 Drama with Immigrants

Many teachers will have shared my feelings of complete
bewilderment and helplessness when first faced with a large
remedial class representing sixteen nationalities. In it there were
recent arrivals, first-generation immigrants and a collection of
English children vaguely labelled "dim."

This situation is commonplace in many of our schools and has
unfortunately led to over-simplifications — the use of the
blanket term "immigrant," for example, to describe those
from backgrounds other than English. Our education system
in its present form finds it difficult to cater for the difficulties
of a rural child facing urbanization, or a working-class child
having to adjust to a predominantly middle-class group, let
alone the many cultural and religious differences among
immigrants.

I am not suggesting that drama is a magic cure-all but I do
believe that it has an important contribution to make in both
understanding of the cross-cultural viewpoint and give the
problems. The use of a framework that by its very nature
encourages flexibility of ideas will facilitate the leader's
understanding of the cross-cultural viewpoint and give the
pupils a mobile means of exploring and adjusting to their new
situation. But the leader concerned must first consider whether
his own attitudes are too fixed to allow for change of attitude
within his group. Or will he distort the situation by being
"over fair" to the black children? Will he remain completely
neutral or will he state his own attitudes if asked by the
group? With such a thorny subject the leader is advised to
do a little soul-searching and maybe take steps to come to
terms with his difficulties — such as a staff-room debate
or even an adult psychodrama group.

Most importantly, he must be **aware** that his bias exists, because only then can he avoid being ruled by it.

Teachers generally consider that language learning is the most acute of all the immigrant's problems. But should we consider language in isolation? Surely it is a part of the total problem of social and emotional adjustment to life in this country? In learning the native language, immigrant children will be exposed not only to new words, but also to concepts they have never come across before — what do a knife and fork mean if you have never seen, let alone used them? Here, creative play can initiate groups into experiences which are taken for granted by most English children. At the same time, it must not have overtones of "our way is better/more civilized than yours!"

Quite apart from the many difficulties of adjusting to a new situation, nowadays referred to as "culture shock" — the immigrant's problems are increased by racial prejudice in his class, at home or on the part of those in authority. A dramatic situation can be used effectively to look at racial prejudice both in the school and in society as a whole.

Additionally, immigrant children have to cope with conflicts between home and school life, particularly when there is a large difference between home and school norms of, for example, eating, dress, manners or discipline. Many children find difficulty in playing this dualistic role. Again, the drama situation can help by allowing the immigrant's culture to come into school — accounts of life in their own countries, performance of songs and dances will give the newcomers a sense of pride in their own heritage, and may help to change the attitudes of their English classmates. The consideration of African, Caribbean or South American influences on our own music and dance forms can show the valid contribution immigrant cultures have made in the past and give English children a chance to re-think their traditional stereotypes. Watching a "live" performance makes an immediate impact, not possible with film and television.

The suggestions in this chapter by no means constitute a blueprint for handling all immigrant classes — this will of course vary according to area, composition of class (i.e. whether children of the same nationality, mixed immigrants, or English as well). There may also be remedial problems and handicaps which occur among immigrants as with other groups, so material in other chapters is also relevant, particularly that in Chapter 9.

One of my first difficulties was that of communicating an attitude of understanding and acceptance without appearing patronizing. I found, furthermore, that in my enthusiasm to give the immigrant children a fair share of attention I was depriving the English children of sufficient recognition. Largely through trial and error with my early groups I arrived at the following aims:

(a) Enlarging the cross-cultural experience of all members of the group, including the leader, through improvisation, projects, etc., based on religious and cultural festivals, dances, songs and stories. This gives each nationality a chance to have status in its own right, as well as having cross feed-back between different cultures.

(b) Providing the opportunity for immigrants to learn:

English norms and conventions, without implying an obligation that they must accept these.

Externalizing and examining social problems such as prejudice between the different groups.

Externalizing feelings that the immigrants have about themselves.

Learning about English law, national and local government, statutory rights, welfare services, job possibilities, etc.

Helping the basic learning process of language.

Guidelines

Infant groups
Swap nursery songs and playground games — for example, "1, 2, 3" (in Greek) turned out to be the Cypriot version of "My Grandmother's Footsteps."

Remember that many immigrant children have to be taught how to play — the whole concept may be new to them.

Juniors
A general geography lesson beginning, "I was born
in. . . and I now live in. . . ."

Dramatize stories from each culture and compare
similarities and differences.

Use music and dance in the same way; many children
know their own folk dances and benefit from teaching
these to other members of the group (don't let the
English children miss out on this).

Improvise "street" scenes, about how the children
live (it is important to know whether they live with
many others from their own country, in a truly mixed
neighbourhood, or are very much in the minority).

Improvise "shopping." Let each nationality take a
turn at leading others, i.e. expedition to Greek shop,
Indian shop, etc. Make up shopping lists and discuss
the things bought — material to make national clothes,
etc.

From above, possibly lead in to cross-cultural cooking —
encourage parents to help with recipes.

Combine several of the above elements to hold a cross-
cultural celebration, or let each culture have its own
festival. Encourage parents to help with costumes,
records, etc. Some background research may be
necessary as many children are hazy about their own
cultures — or else don't like to admit that they know.

Remember that many of the songs and dances are
religious and should therefore be treated with the
same deference as an improvisation of a Church of
England Christening or a Roman Catholic Mass.

Teenage groups
Dance drama.

Dramatized debates.

Playmaking around social themes.

Projects around history, economics and politics.

Let the class be representatives of the United Nations.

Improvise/debate around themes from daily newspapers concerning particular countries.

For all groups: Remember that a voluntary helper who is also an immigrant can make very valuable contributions.

Practical Illustrations
1   Recently I had to work purely on intuition with a group of Indian girls newly arrived in this country from Gujerat. The harassed headmistress had simply said, "Do something, anything!"

The girls knew only a handful of English words; they huddled together on a bench in the vast games hall, either giggling nervously or looking far away, shut off from the immediate environment. I began by trying out various types of music, including lively beaty rhythms for clapping, but there was no reaction. Musical instruments, glove puppets and stimulating pictures were treated with the same indifference. Eventually I played a record of traditional Indian music and immediately saw a positive response from the whole group. Previously glazed eyes became animated and, after a few nudges and a whispered conversation, the girls got up and did a folk dance together, feeling a little self-conscious and looking at me anxiously to see my reaction. After a while I tried to copy them and proved a poor pupil; this caused much laughter and released the tension. We then got down to business and I was taught their dance.

The following week I suggested that they brought their saris to school; I brought mine and they showed me how to wear it. This developed into a mini-festival when the girls also brought chapatis from home. Later, the group was able to generalize into new experiences. The girls were by then quite happy to learn dances from me, and I deliberately made use of contrast to complement their soft flowing movement — we did a very energetic Spanish finger-clicking dance.

The important factor seemed to be that they had something

to teach me and furthermore it was "all right" to do it at school. We did similar swapping of songs and slowly progressed to language learning by using the words of the songs and painting the stories of the songs.

2 Of all the children referred to me for therapy, the biggest proportion have been West Indians deemed to be "physically out of control" by Western standards or "violently acting out." It seemed necessary to utilize this physical energy and native skill in body co-ordination. Many enjoyed dancing and drumming to beaty music but others, usually top juniors upwards, were more reluctant to

respond and the most usual scene was a brawling pile of bodies on the floor, or hands in pockets and mute sulking, or "We're only going to come if we can play football."

I used many of the children's games as starters, such as "Sticky Toffee," which turned out to be off-the-ground chain tig of my own playground days! We began swapping games and I quickly adapted certain encounter-group techniques and relabelled them, e.g. "Break the Circle," where all the group except one stand in a tight circle, arms round each other's shoulders, while the person outside tries to break into the middle. This was a very popular game; as well as channelling physical energy it was useful in providing opportunities for physical contact that were not babyish.

With these same groups I used sword-fighting with masks and fencing sabres and stick-fighting with broomsticks, though naturally not putting weapons in their hands if they were already out of control. Having channelled the interest into a specific physical activity a fight could then be placed in the wider context of a story such as Robin Hood or one which we invented.

Since football is so popular I have frequently used it to begin a session and developed it in various ways: initially having a real ball and then not, using it in slow motion, action replays, orchestrating football songs, commentators, interviews, court cases following disturbances, footballers being auctioned for transfer to new clubs, TV quiz games, fan letters. One project received a great impetus when a Brazilian voluntary helper joined the group and the boys were quite certain that she was "Pele's wife or something."

Many of the above suggestions can help to stimulate language and fluency, particularly if one has the use of a cassette tape-recorder for "the BBC creep doing interviews" and a solid old desk-typewriter for writing newsflashes and fan letters.

3 I was asked by a teacher in a special language unit for young immigrants to devise creative games to reinforce her lessons.

Using familiar tunes I adapted singing games for teaching right and left, large and small, with movement to accompany specific words. We used movement, sound and stories with sound effects to facilitate consonants and vowels. My imagination was taxed to the full as the story of the "snake that went sssssss in the forest of whispering trees" (all whispering sounds that we orchestrated), and "the 'blurp' machine in the magic factory" became firm favourites. There was also a magic pool where some strange creatures lived called the ka-kas and the quee-quees. The possibilities for facilitating language learning in this way are endless.

4 Drama and the Backward Child

Although creative drama is becoming more integrated into education programmes as a whole it is still used remarkably little with remedial groups in ordinary schools, special schools for the educationally subnormal and junior training centres (the latter having recently become the responsibility of the Education instead of Health Authority).

When visiting schools I have been rather dismayed at how often I am asked to work with bright groups, with the comment, "Well, of course, the others would be hopeless at it." While firmly believing that all groups should have drama I would say that, if it is a question of choice, the slow-learning groups should have priority. Another curious misconception about drama is that only the bright children can be truly imaginative; I have often found the reverse, that the response of bright groups tends to be highly conventional and unoriginal while the groups of those of lesser academic ability have fewer preconceived ideas of what they "should" do.

When working as a class teacher in an ESN school I used drama as the focus from which other learning activities grew. As I was also taking the other classes in the school for drama I found the co-operation of the staff invaluable in shaping an integrated programme, incorporating all other subjects; and it was here that drama as a learning medium could really be explored. Although an end-of-term concert was expected, I had the headmaster's sanction to break away from more formal presentations; we were able to develop for performance themes which had been worked on during the term in improvisation and projects. Because of the flexibility of the school itself one could really say that drama "worked" at many levels and in different ways. For example, when a dance session for the senior girls, who had wanted to learn a can-can, was being rudely gawped and whistled at by older boys peering through the windows I was able to bring the boys into the session and stage a French nightclub scene where they drank champagne out of the girls' slippers. Similarly, one of the infant classes sent a deputation to say "We've been practising the can-can in the playground, can we do it as well?"

Care had to be taken with older groups in choosing material that was on the one hand sophisticated enough but on the other not too abstract. Sword-fighting, as described in Chapter 3, was used extensively and developed into pageants, simulated wrestling and boxing matches. The senior boys in particular liked to improvise new instalments of television serials. The girls benefited greatly from doing dances like the can-can, for which they industriously sewed garters, and "kicking" routines which developed their co-ordination and had a marked effect on their confidence and personality — droopy shoulders seemed to grow inches taller, especially when lank hair was chignonned on top.

Guidelines

Do not despair at an unpredictable response; for example when I asked one group what a particular piece of evocative music sounded like, one girl answered, "A few violins and a trumpet."

Choose ideas from within the group's own experience and extend them. For instance, a school journey, say to a castle, could enrich the content of a subsequent drama lesson (before this approach became routine, one child said to me, "I hate going on outings, because you have to come back and write about them").

Unexpected situations can often provoke unforeseen developments! I was practising sword-play with a class of eleven-year-old ESN boys, took the sword above my head and brought down a large glass light-fitting. As I passed out (literally) I heard

one voice say, "Cor, you've killed Miss." This
developed into a hospital improvisation.

ESN groups respond well to drama projects around
educational themes that are part of the normal
curricula. Utilize the drama session in particular
for teaching first-aid, road safety, the use of public
telephones, dialling 999 — emphasizing the importance of clear simple speech.

Use verbal situations outside their immediate experience to enlarge vocabulary.

Always keep in mind the use of drama for helping
these children to be more self-reliant and indepen-
dent.

Practical Illustrations
1 A class of twelve ESN boys in a day school, with a wide
variety of backgrounds and capabilities.
Cowboys were the favourite theme so we transformed the
classroom into a Western saloon with posters and record
sleeves. The class were quite willing to sit quietly for more
formal learning when dressed up in check shirts, necker-
chieves and simulated bruises and black eyes done with
blackboard chalk. Ordinary timetable subjects went on in
this environment — linked to cowboys when possible and
then occasional breaks for drama. In maths we were counting
heads of cattle, wages, betting odds, etc.
I alternated the cowboy music on the record player
between lulling tunes such as "The Lavender Cowboy" and
more stimulating rhythms, such as "Jesse James" if the class got
too sleepy. At the end of the day we would sing "Get along
little dogies" round the camp fire.
Improvisation developed around Western themes and the
class showed a high degree of physical control and dexterity as they learned to leap from imaginary horses, threw
each other across saloon tables and did "dive" falls backwards out of the windows. The situations were very stylized
so a mock fight never became a fight for real. They were
always well balanced with quieter, relaxed periods. (These

exercises grew from the classic "stage fall," i.e. fall on to knees, then hip before lying flat. This should be practised slowly at first and gradually speeded up until the movements follow without a break. The fall can then be varied. N.B. It can also be used for teaching relaxation.)

In contrast to the highly energetic aspect of this theme we developed a great deal of singing, painting and writing.

2 Christmas concert with all the senior end of the school, for the entertainment of parents and school manager.

I refused to select only certain children as performers and said it was all or nobody. I blackmailed the staff into joining in also.

During the term we had been working on themes and variations around the sea and the concert was to be a nautical evening. It started with sea-shanties round a bar piano, all the sailors wearing teeshirts and jeans and sporting enormous beards. This helped even the most nervous child to feel at home.

To "H.M.S. Pinafore" music the boys swabbed the decks, loaded the ship and set off to sea. Their mission was to find Black Jake, a pirate on the high seas. Black Jake was sighted, the grappling irons were put on and deck-to-deck combat ensued. Then a storm blew up ("Ride of the Valkyries," thunder sheet, lightning effects). The ships sank and the crews swam for shore. They were washed up on a deserted island ("Fingal's Cave"). The crews got together and said they would follow whichever leader, i.e. Black Jake or the Captain, won a duel. Captain Carston (of course) won and the story ended with Black Jake's funeral and the crew starting to build a new ship to sail home. There was hilarity after Black Jake's dying wound when one boy turned the body over and said in a loud whisper, "Show the blood to the audience" (we had previously made a large simulated wound with stage blood under Black Jake's shirt).

We had a closing scene of the arrival back in port and then finished off the first half of the programme with hornpipe dances, first seriously by the girls and then a comedy act by the boys (tripping over their feet, losing their trousers, showing bright red long-johns, etc.).

The audience absorbtion was tremendous, particularly during the deck-to-deck fighting — we had managed to beg some wax bottles which broke like glass and greatly heightened the effect.

The second half opened with an underwater fantasy scene using ultra-violet lighting. The woodwork teacher and his class had constructed very simple but effective rocks, and among them treasure chests cascading dubloons, painted in ultra-violet sensitive paint. When the curtain went up it looked truly magic. To the accompaniment of weird electronic music a group dressed all in black manipulated enormous cut-outs of underwater creatures - fishes, octopuses — in and out of the caverns.

The evening ended with more sea-shanties with audience participation. Encores abounded and there was a sense of well-being and achievement on everybody's part. The only disaster came when I attempted to remove the beards which I had *glued* on the Headmaster and a teacher — I had forgotten that both these men had well-cultivated sideboards!

5 Drama with the Disturbed, Maladjusted and Psychotic

"I've been sent to you because I've got problems — but I'd rather do some drama"! This statement from one youngster at a drama session highlights the current trend for using drama only to diagnose and examine problems, thus neglecting the therapeutic value of creativity itself. It is understandable that, when a drama specialist is asked to justify the use of his techniques he should emphasize "problem drama" since the more nebulous "healing factor" in creativity is difficult to define or measure scientifically.

However, it is frequently apparent from observation of groups and individuals after creative sessions that significant changes have taken place. A totally fragmented group may achieve a feeling of unity (extremely beneficial for the child who has never "belonged"), or a tense and inhibited child may become relaxed and peaceful, without necessarily giving the leader any clues as to the cause of his distress. I would emphasize that the leader must sense when direct probing is inappropriate. It is naturally tempting to want everything neat and tidy, with causes identified and effects noted, but the therapeutic session is rarely that. Much goes on "inside" that at most the leader can only guess.

On some points it is possible to be more specific; a person may find relief in being able to express distorted fantasies without guilt or fear of judgement. It can be helpful *not* to focus on a particular problem and thereby reinforce the "normal" aspects.

Unfortunately, in the past, harm has been done when drama was used with disturbed groups without sufficient forethought. Chaotic consequences have ensued, for instance, when highly stimulating activities have been used with an already stimulated group. It is essential with such groups, especially in the early sessions, to provide a secure framework, where boundaries are firm. The reference earlier in this book to the use of ritual is very relevant here, as are the suggestions for boundarying stimulation within calmness and relaxation.

Having stated briefly the particular value of drama for these groups and given some indication of the form of drama which is most effective, i.e. flexible but boundaried, I propose to offer ideas (which have all been tried) for use not only in Special Schools and Child Guidance Clinics but also by the teacher working with difficult groups in ordinary classroom situations. When we consider one of the schools with which I have been personally involved, with a remedial intake of 40 per cent, it is clear that teachers must have help in coping with what is by no means a minority problem.

Much of a preventive nature can be done through drama. By mobilizing creative skills we may well be resolving problems before they become too extreme. Furthermore, through the varied nature of dramatic work, it is sometimes possible to discover the individual "at risk." This is frequently the case with the withdrawn child, often considered to be just quiet, shy or well behaved. It is significant that at least three-quarters of the problem children referred to me were the class-disrupters, violent and noisy. On further investigation it was apparent that there were many children considered "abnormally quiet" but they would at least sit still.

Many teachers have said to me, "We could cope with problem children in our classes if only the classes were smaller," or "I can't let the whole class suffer by giving one group too much attention." This is reality and I cannot pretend that drama will radically change it. However, some of the following ideas can help contain a problem situation, or can provide intermediate relief until more specialized help is available. This can be critical when, as frequently happens, a child has to wait a long time for referral, transfer or even assessment.

Guidelines
(especially for disturbed and maladjusted groups; also see Chapter 10 on Psychodrama and Role-playing)

> When planning sessions be sure to liaise with other specialists such as Child Guidance Staff. Be careful not

to give out nebulous ideas; always start with a clear, firm base such as dance-movement to favourite music — even violent teenage groups have responded to such pieces of music as "The Stripper" or "The Magnificent Seven" and even interpreted the "Avengers" theme music through improvised modern ballet.

Establish security by use of ritual through movement or situations, such as favourite stories or situations; or even an improvisation around a theme of security and safety.

Opportunities to play out home situations — family breakfast, rows with Dad — are welcome providing they are done naturally within the drama framework and not staged with an attitude of "We're here to look at your problems."

Contrast the above with themes removed from the group's own experience — outer space, underwater. People will still frequently "play themselves" whatever the theme but may feel safer if another dimension, such as masks, is added.

With a very disturbed group try the "Safe Circle": suggest that each person is enclosed in a circle (chalked on floor if necessary) which is his own and safe; outside the circle is alien territory which can be explored at will, either alone or in pairs — it can be deserted, spooky, crowded, etc.

Bring in as much physical touch as possible.

Beware of imposing end-of-session discussion — allow it to occur spontaneously if the group so wish. Time to consolidate a profound experience is often needed.

Bear in mind that the session must involve above all else caring and acceptance on the part of the leader.

Practical Illustrations
A group of twenty girls, aged 15 to 18, in a girls' approved school. The girls had been in the school for periods of time ranging

from two years to a matter of weeks. Although I knew they were there for a wide variety of reasons, I was unfortunately not allowed details of individual case histories. In one or two instances I was simply told that the background was "not very nice."

On the first visit attendance was voluntary and about a third of the girls initially participated. At first they were extremely shy and seemed to expect that excessive demands would be made on them. However, these fears were soon dispelled with simple dance movement and body warm-ups. Little by little other girls came into the room on various pretexts until we were working with the full number.

We developed extensive movement into a simple dance routine to "Georgy Girl" which was built up slowly in progressions.

Verbal work started with simple word improvisations rather like extended charades — there was a strong response to the word "Protest" which developed spontaneously into a full-scale project and included demonstrations, freedom marching, soap-box oratory, clashes with the law and their outcome, where the girls showed remarkable eloquence.

The session lasted for 2½ hours; it was marked by all the girls' sheer enjoyment of participating in such activity and their eagerness to continue.

A few months later an intensive weekend course was arranged. The girls learned a wide range of international dances — can-can, gypsy dance and a military routine — and these were to be integrated into an international festival taking place in a village in India. With the help of visual aids the problems of India were discussed in a group session, with all the girls contributing their own ideas. It was apparent in these discussions that the girls' factual knowledge was extremely limited and there was a feeling that the topic was geographical and unrelated to them personally. However, that initial resistance was quickly overcome by posters which included — The Taj Mahal, various scenes of Indian mythology, costumes, dance and village life. A member of staff was able to produce enough traditional saris for the girls to wear and they were taught a very simple classical Indian dance wearing them. In saris the girls, many of whom were awkward and over-weight, were able to move with beauty and co-ordination.

After concentration on dancing, we began to work at a deeper

level. A real interest was shown in the human aspects — the
poverty, starvation, disease and other social problems in India. It
was obvious that many of the girls were identifying very much
with these problems.

The girls worked in groups with different community roles
such as rice-planters, tea-pickers, grain-guards, etc. They developed
this themselves into a riot on the grain towers as a rebellion
against the rice queues and subsequent wastage of grain, a plague
of rats, an influx of disease, several deaths which invocation of
the gods could not prevent, and then a return to the old way of
life.

Guidelines (especially for psychotics)

Remember that one is attempting to bring the individual
"in touch" with himself so that he may experience himself as a whole person — physically, mentally and
emotionally.

Use a large hoop to encompass leader and child, or a
long piece of ribbon held at each end, as a means of
keeping in touch "at a distance"; gradually narrow the
distance between leader and child if this is tolerated.
Long stretches of ribbon/paper can also be used to dance
with — for encouraging extended large movement. (Many
psychotics flick ribbons, etc., anyway, so make use of
this.)

Paired bongo drums are very effective when working
with an individual — shared non-verbal communication
can be established and frequently eye contact develops
as patient becomes absorbed in activity.

Try making use of child's rocking and sound patterns —
as suggested in Chapter 7.

Use regular simple rhythms in percussion, singing and
music to establish "patterns."

Use singing and action games that mention body parts
to help body awareness and identity.

Sometimes an individual, if not pressed, will spontaneously join in activities such as shadow puppets or finger-painting.

Make use of boxes, paper sacks for getting inside.

Build movement progressions from marching, side-stepping in a circle into simple dances.

Use as many voluntary helpers as possible to increase staff ratio, to help children integrate in a group — though sometimes it is necessary to work individually.

Practical Illustrations

1 An autistic unit. Sessions were rather spasmodic as the unit was newly formed, and children were being sent and then transferred.

Unless I had student helpers, it was difficult to work with more than one or two children at a time because while I was helping one, the others would be spinning on one toe or flicking in a corner or dismantling the record-player!

The best solution was for me to sit on the floor with one child on my lap and hold hands with the rest. We did rocking and swaying to music and gradually the group tolerated contact for longer and longer without trying to break away. We progressed into simple clapping — one, two, one two — where I made a point of always saying the words as well as doing the action in order to encourage speech: Simple movement followed, again with words: "We go up very tall, then down very small, and now we roll over and over."

I used a great deal of movement to make different shapes — circles, lines — with different body parts as well as doing whole body movement in circles and lines on the floor.

2 Many of the above techniques I modified when working in a psychiatric hospital with adult psychotics in a long-term ward. We always began with movement in a circle and simple dances. Miming of familiar objects and then using them — marbles, beach balls — developed new movement and stimulated interest. As much as possible I used activities to involve the whole group at the same time, such as all of us lifting a grand piano or heaving

a large boulder; this was more successful than small group
activity, where interest was quickly lost and people drifted away.
Drumming, either with instruments or on chairs, was very
popular at each session and facilitated a big build-up of feeling
and tension, followed by gradual relaxation again.

6 Drama with the Physically Handicapped

The range of physical disability is very wide and includes both impairment of a sense, as with the deaf or blind, and extreme forms of handicap, where several if not all limbs are incapacitated. The special problems of these three conditions will be considered in later sections of this chapter, although leaders will be able to adapt material from other sections to their own particular group. Those working with the multiply handicapped should also refer to Chapter 7.

Excellent ideas have been pioneered by Pat Keysell with "The National Theatre of the Deaf," but the use of drama with the physically handicapped is still in its infancy. Some have been confused into thinking that movement therapy is like physio-therapy — "What is the necessity for additional treatment if a school or hospital already has a physiotherapist?" We must distinguish clearly between movement as a part of drama, and the manipulation techniques for corrective movement and inhibiting faulty response, which are the highly specialized skills of the physiotherapist. One physiotherapist put it to me that drama could encourage faulty movement. I suggested that if drama could be used to motivate generalized movement initially, then later the "right" movements could be reinforced. The important contribution of drama is that it can take the focus off the physical handicap, an approach similar to using non-verbal communication with the child with speech difficulties. Children have been known to attempt completely new movements spon-taneously while absorbed in an exciting theme. (One child stood for the first time during one of our mime games; a member of staff cried ,"Look, Sally's standing!" whereupon Sally promptly sat down again and did not attempt to get up for another week or so.)

49

I have run training courses specifically for physiotherapists in creative techniques which they have adapted to their own approach; a most exciting venture was working with a physiotherapist on a collaborative programme for wheelchair children. For those working in the field of gross handicap I would suggest that the ideas should not be attempted without previous consultation with the physiotherapist or doctor.

Drama can be used to help come to terms with additional problems such as those caused by early hospitalization. We must not neglect, either, the emotional difficulties of the individual who is physically disabled but intelligent and very aware of his "difference."

Some people I have worked with had opted out and become totally lethargic because they felt their handicap too great for them really to belong to society. We must always remember "that anything can be done in drama"; all handicaps can be overcome in fantasy. As one girl from the Belgian Congo, struggling with the twin problems of confinement to a wheel-chair and being the only black girl in the hospital, put it: "For the first time, we're all equal."

Many of those with minimal handicaps are now integrated into ordinary classroom situations and can derive satisfaction from joining in ordinary activities, including drama. One such child proved highly inventive in an improvisation about the sea in which he very ingeniously used his crutches as the rudder of the boat.

THE BLIND

With the blind and partially sighted, drama may be used to develop the other senses, in particular hearing and touch, as well as to encourage confidence in mobility. Many blind people feel disoriented in space; to remedy this I frequently start with work on the floor. It provides a firm, safe base and minimizes the chances of falling or colliding with people and things. From sitting or lying on the floor the group can progress to kneeling, crouching and standing — let the group experiment with crossing space from a low position, such as hands and knees, before the more complex actions of walking, running or dancing.

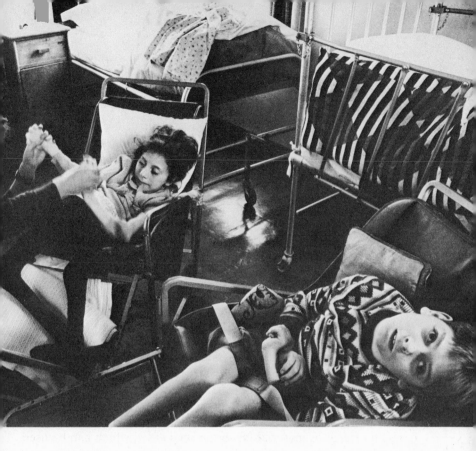

Guidelines

Use the relaxation and warm-up techniques described in Chapter 2, with the group seated on the floor in a circle.

Work in pairs, partners holding hands and swaying, to stimulate trust.

Use as many textures of movement as possible: "Sit very stiff, move your arms like flowing water/sea waves/like a boxer."

Encourage awareness of movement by simple occupational mimes — stirring, kneading, cutting, writing, telephoning, etc. Remember that the early sessions will have to be very simple and directive, often with close physical help from the leader to demonstrate movements and actions that are not clear.

Explore movement shapes such as lines, circles, figures of eight, from a static seated or standing position before developing patterns in the room.

Environmental work with things to explore, go through and under, as well as interesting textures to handle, is very rewarding.

Develop the use of sounds and sound effects as early as possible.

Use themes where the handicap does not intrude — exploring pitch-dark underwater caverns.

THE DEAF

Mime and movement really come into their own with the deaf and partially hearing and such work does require an ability on the part of the leader to express himself through these means. Care must be taken to complement the highly specific movement needed for mimed communication with large free-flowing whole body expression.

Although the leader's task is in some ways simplified by the greater range of material (such as visual aids), which can be used with deaf groups, compared with the blind, there tend to be more emotional frustrations with which deaf people have to come to terms. Particularly acute are feelings of isolation accentuated by being able to see other people communicating but being unable to understand what's going on. Group participation in drama does help to alleviate some of these problems.

All the suggestions for non-verbal work can be adapted for deaf groups.

Guidelines

Physical contact is important.

Encourage accuracy of mime to facilitate communication which can otherwise be hazy and non-specific.

Encourage the expression of *feelings* through sound as well as movement — laughter and fears need to be expressed.

Remember there are situations where nobody can hear anyway! Underwater or on a busy building site.

Although speech work will often be rudimentary it should nevertheless be encouraged together with sound improvisations.

Many deaf people, though unable to hear music, can sense rhythm and pulsation — floors and furniture as well as percussion instruments can be used to transmit vibrations.

OTHER HANDICAPS

Work developed with groups in wheelchairs has been one of the most rewarding challenges I have undertaken. In several institutions on fine days the chairs were wheeled on to balconies or into the garden but otherwise there was only the television room to alleviate the boredom between mealtimes, doctors' visits and physiotherapy sessions. Almost all the normal activities were of a passive "watching" nature, and staff were initially sceptical about drama actually "working."

Ideas evolved, not only for things that could be done sitting in wheelchairs (which of course were very similar to other sitting drama activities) but also where the wheelchair itself could be utilized. During warm-up sessions the wheelchair is useful for making sound effects with feet and hands. Several chairs grouped in pairs behind each other became all types of vehicle including trains and space ships, making a point of utilizing as many knobs and dials already there as possible. But it really came into its own as a dodgem car during a fairground improvisation. Lengths of cloth were draped round the lower part of the chair and the girls were able to simulate ladies dancing in crinolines. Visual aids helped here — they showed African dancers and Kathakali Indian dancers wearing long padded bell-skirts, so the boys in the group felt it was perfectly manly to dance too. Full-length mirrors borrowed from the physiotherapy department were invaluable, particularly when the group wore make-up or masks (acquired from the Commonwealth Institute archives). Although masks and make-up will be discussed more fully in Chapter 11, I must make a special note of how important they were with these groups. Children, previously apathetic and unresponsive,

completely changed when allowed to put on their own make-up.
One child took twenty minutes to become a clown, holding a
stick of greasepaint in one hand and guiding the movements by
holding her wrist with her other hand as she strove for sym-
metry. Her tremendous pleasure in doing this emphasized how
essential it was to encourage individuals to do things for themselves or for each other, rather than let staff step in because it
was quicker.

Guidelines

Never underestimate the dramatic possibilities with
these groups.

Think in terms of a wheelchair as an alternative to feet;
immediately many more things become possible, such
as marching, dancing.

When possible, enlist the help of more mobile children
to facilitate processions and more ambitious wheelchair
movement.

Make use of gently rocking the wheelchair to induce
calmness and relaxation.

Include as much rhythmic work as you can in music and
movement, as so many of these children have become
"out of rhythm" as a result of their handicaps.

This in turn will facilitate better co-ordination (make
use of natural rhythms such as heartbeats, taps dripping,
axes chopping).

Practical Illustrations

1 Group of fifteen children, aged 9 to 12, hospitalized since
infancy in a 2,000-bed institution in Germany.

We chose a circus theme, because a touring circus had recently
visited the hospital and the children were still talking about it.

After an initial warm-up we used circus activities for the whole
group before subdividing into smaller group work. We began with
a large march, with real and mimed musical instruments. (Tapes
and records of traditional circus music were of course essential.)
Then everybody became elephants and we used hoops over the

backs of wheelchairs, held by the person in the chair behind, to
link up in true elephant follow-my-leader fashion. Two of the
staff made archways for the procession to go through. We went
on to horses and experimented with typical head movements
for a horse wearing plumes, again linking wheelchairs for the
horses to move in formation. Some of the staff "rode" on the
chairs like bareback riders. This developed spontaneously into
a Wild West scene, with cowboys and Indians and much whoop-
ing and gunfire.

For contrast we tried something much slower and sustained:
a simple chalk-line drawn across the floor was enough to provoke
the idea of tightrope walkers and trapeze artistes. Wheelchairs
were pushed slowly along the line while the occupant feigned
loss of balance or dread of heights. The idea of balancing objects
while on the tightrope evolved and the children walked the rope
again with long canes with plastic mugs on top. Next they tried
group crossing, linking themselves by hoops and canes, with
storms of applause from the rest of the group awaiting their
turn.

Change of mood again, as we introduced clowns, initially
just doing funny things and practical jokes while pulling "rubber"
faces; later we introduced make-up. A few simple aids, like a
plastic bucket filled with torn-up paper, were enough to set the
scene; the wheelchairs were ideal for simulating the classic
clowns' car that won't go.

We split into smaller groups and each chose their own activity;
all groups tried out a whole range of circus acts before choosing
a favourite. The children said they wanted to invite people to
their circus, so we arranged for some more children, visiting
students and hospital staff to come.

The group received their guests at the door, showed them to
their seats, sold ice-creams and popcorn with mimed skill and
we ran through a whole performance beginning and ending with
a grand march. The "audience" joined in the final march and it
developed into a lively conga taking people back to their respect-
ive wards and offices.

2 Group of twelve adolescent girls in a residential school for
the physically handicapped.

This was a once-only visit, to illustrate for staff how drama

could be used. I and three students had worked out a broad
journey framework, whereby we would travel to special places
by means of a magic carpet. We used the usual warm-up plus
some concentrated mime work as we prepared for the journey.
I told the main points of the story as we went along, but
frequently stopped for discussion/decision-making by the group.
Framework: Countries to be visited — the Land of Sea and
Shells, the Land of Mud Puddles, the Land of Witches and the
Land of Princesses.
Necessary equipment: A large rug, as a magic carpet, a telescope,
a large number of very beautiful shells and seaside objects,
theatrical crowns and jewellery, records — sea sound effects,
electronic bubbly music, spooky music and mediaeval dance
music.
     We introduced ourselves to the group and got to know their
names. We told them that we were going on a journey to find a
lost treasure-chest. Having assembled on the magic carpet we all
had to think of the magic word that would make it fly. Once
airborne we described what we could see and the girl with the
telescope said she could see an island. Once the magic word had
been found we landed in the Land of Sea and Shells (sound
effects) where we explored. There were beautiful shells to
listen to and handle and one turned out to be magic — possibly
it could help us out of any trouble.
     We set off again and arrived in the Land of Mud Puddles
where we had great difficulty getting ourselves through a black
slough and had to help each other from sinking right in, but it
was the only way to get to the next part of our journey. When
we got to the Land of Witches we washed in the river, generally
cleaned up and lit a fire to dry ourselves. While one member of
the group was foraging for wood she reported strange happenings
in the wood (begin sound effects). The girls spontaneously became witches and put dreadful spells on all the staff, brewing
potions for a really terrible spell to deal with the headmaster.
Luckily the magic shell enabled the witches to turn back into
themselves and we all went in search of our magic carpet,
realizing that it had been left behind in Mud Puddle Land.
Miraculously the magic shell helped again and we took off for
the Land of Princesses.
     There were celebrations going on at the Court when we

arrived and everybody was invited to join in. However, we had no princess clothes to wear, so regretfully refused and went on with our search for the treasure-chest. With the help of the magic shell and a kindly old crone we came to the tree where the chest was buried; we dug it up, to find it was enormous. We all dressed up in the beautiful crowns, necklaces and earrings we found inside. Then of course we were quite properly dressed for going back to the Court and we danced very dignified court dances with bows and curtsies. After drinking a royal toast, it was time to go home. We put all the treasures back in the chest and carried it with great effort on to magic carpet. It was a very long journey back and we slept all the way before touching down home. Curiously, when we woke up the magic shell had disappeared.

This story sequence was very important for this particular group and helped them in several different ways. They were able to dance with partners despite their wheel chairs. Many of the girls were very ashamed of their looks so to be able to dress up, not just as ordinary people but as princesses, was a very special experience. The particular clothes — well-made theatrical costumes, borrowed from a drama school — helped tremendously. Too, the girls were able to be in control as well as expressing hostile feelings when inventing the magic spells. Not least, the fantasy elements of the magic carpet enabled them to move outside their own bodies which, they were only too well aware, were less than perfect.

7 Drama with the Severely Subnormal and Multiply Handicapped

The frustration and despair of parents, nurses and teachers working long term with the severely handicapped is easy to understand but difficult to resolve. The daily routine of physical care such as feeding, dressing and washing is time-consuming and extremely demanding, increasingly so as the child grows physically larger. Hospital staff have the additional problems of overcrowding and a daily routine with very little light or shade.

Many specialists in education and health, while accepting the importance of drama with school groups, have felt it to be inappropriate in the fields of gross handicap. The relaxed laughing faces of both staff and children during a recent session in a severe subnormality unit, when the consultant paediatrician was sitting on the floor playing "talking toes" with matron (see Chapter 11), were enough to convince me that there are no physical or mental barriers to participating in drama.

With the severely impaired child there is a complex problem: that of the damage, possibly both mental and physical, and the emotional disturbance frequently resulting from early hospitalization or misguided handling at home. It is easy to forget that however severe the handicap, such children's emotional needs are as strong as or stronger than those of a normal child. It is not that these children cannot communicate but that their means of communication are limited. Rarely will speech be acquired and therefore non-verbal communication using movement and sound can enable feelings of love, hate and sadness to be expressed.

Furthermore, creative techniques can provide situations for group interaction between children and adults. Many of the following suggestions can be incorporated into a daily ward routine, and if half an hour's "special time" can be set aside

59

this is better still. Above all it should be fun, not only for the
children but for the staff as well.

Guidelines

Many wards already have piped music and this can be
used for relaxing movement or more stimulating activities.
Even children confined permanently to cots will have at
least one limb that can be moved in time to music,
whether it is a soft slow waving or faster rhythmic
tapping.

Hospital equipment often includes toys to jingle or
bang tied to the cots. Try using these in a group activity
where *everybody* makes a lot of noise and then a little
sound, or plays them very quickly and then very slowly.
Cot bars and wheelchairs make useful percussion instruments, too. The leader should try to go to each member
of the group and do the activity with them, if only
briefly.

Simple exercises using physical contact are invaluable to
mobilize lethargic limbs. With adult and even geriatric
subnormal groups, movement to music is important to
counteract premature inactivity.

If time is at a premium, nursery rhymes, singing games
and action songs can be done during nappy-changing or
meal times. One German institution I worked in had a
special song that the staff and children sang or hummed
before lunch.

There is a wealth of singing games with very simple tunes
and actions. Popular songs and ballads, with appropriate
movements, can be added to the fund of nursery rhymes
that we all know.
    Example: "He's got the whole world in his hands."
These actions were thought out by a group of young
ESN children and were then used with SSN children:

He's got the whole world in his hands . . . (large circle
                      movement, arms opening out)

He's got the wind and the rain . . . (arms up swaying
> side to side)
He's got the little baby . . . (arms cradled side to side)
He's got both you and me . . . (pointing to you and me)
> Clapping the ending.

This song with actions can also be done walking round
the room.

Many staff are naturally distressed by the repetitive
crying, head banging, rocking, etc., so common in subnormal wards. These sounds and movements can be used
and modified by staff sharing the activity and then
varying it. For example, let rocking gradually slow down
or change direction (side to side instead of backwards
and forwards); let crying sounds develop into screaming
sounds and then grow into laughter. Following this, new
movements and sounds can often be introduced.
N.B. It is important that the leader starts from the same
point as the patient and does not attempt to change mood
too quickly. This work must necessarily be individual,
(when children have to be helped to do most of the
actions), but a small group can work together if there
are helpers and in time some group integration can be
attempted.

The following is a typical framework that I have used
with all ages in subnormal wards, and can be adapted
according to whether the groups are mobile, in chairs or
sitting on the floor.

Relaxing
Using gentle and unhurried music, rocking movement holding
hands.
Stretch right up towards the ceiling and come down again.
Use hands and arms in "wave" movements up and down the
sides of the body.
Move heads from side to side.
Sitting on the floor, bend knees up and wrap arms tightly
round, then slowly open out.

Warming-up
Clap simple rhythms to beaty music that is not too fast.
When the rhythm is established the clap can be done over the
head, low down, etc.
Shake hands vigorously one at a time and then together. Again,
vary the direction once the movement is established.
Shrug the shoulders up and down.
Wiggle hips side to side or "like a hula hoop."
Let the fingers dance (or play an imaginary piano).
Alternately lift each elbow.
Shake one foot at a time.
Rise on tiptoes and down.
Bend knees and straighten.

Development
Slap the floor, gradually getting louder and then softer.
March on the spot, into the middle of the circle and out again.
Stamp on the floor, very fast and then very slow.
Using one arm make large circle movements; contrast this by
making tiny circles with finger movement.

Sounds
Blowing — gently and then more vigorously.
Shhh — gently and then more vigorously.
Alternate the two.
Simple consonant sounds — *b, b, baaaaaaaa*
                          c, c, caaaaaaaa
(done to music or with clapping or movement)
Long vowel sounds — *Aaaaaaaaaaaa*
(vary it in shapes and patterns)
Using one of the above sounds at a time, very simple chants can
be built up. Many children cannot make the sound but enjoy
being "in" the experience.

Touch
Touch the surroundings, feeling chairs, floor, hair. . . .
Have a magic box containing things with different textures to be
explored, e.g. velvet, corduroy, polystyrene, shells, wood-bark,
sand, egg-shells. Even if the children are too handicapped to pick
things up, the leader can hold them in the child's hand, against
the soles of the feet.

Finish off the session with a simple action story where everybody joins in the action, such as:

"We were all curled up fast asleep but it was time to get up, so we stretched our arms, yawned and rubbed our eyes . . . it was time to clean teeth . . ." the leader pointing the words by doing the actions very precisely, the group following — later members of the group will initiate actions themselves. (Go through teeth-cleaning sequence in mime, not forgetting finer detail such as remembering to turn the tap off!) This sort of introduction can lead in to a simple surprise — a present to be opened, a special visitor or a walk where various things are found or seen, ending up at the end of the day slowly getting ready for bed, curling up and going to sleep, eyes closed. I find if the final relaxing is done slowly and concentratedly it is possible to get total silence with some of the children actually sleeping. Lack of involvement is indicated by giggling, snorting; if this happens, deliberately encourage giggling for a short time and then let it quieten into sleep.

Practical Illustration

John is a 2½-year-old hydrocephalic wearing a valve but still severely subnormal; on the Griffiths developmental test he was ascertained as functioning at an 8-months old level.

He had been having individual sessions with me for twenty minutes twice a week for two months. He shrank from any physical contact, was unresponsive to most musical sounds and noises and would jump violently and be upset at sudden loud noises. Most of the time he gazed through and beyond me.

I decided to try a variety of touch stimuli and placed various things in his hand such as pebbles and shells, and he dropped them. But when I put egg shells into his hand he held them and crushed them, beaming as he did so. I gave him another and he brought both hands together to crush; he seemed delighted with the noise as well as the feel. When I put bits of dried fern into his hands it stuck to the egg white and he began to rub it off with one finger at a time, exploring his whole hand. Accompanying this were pleasure noises and eye contact with me. Six months later John's range of activities included physical touch, response to singing games, and use of his hands to explore, tearing paper with dogged persistence.

8 Carrying on as Adults?

Many people see the relevance of drama in therapeutic work with children and adolescents but are less convinced of its application to adults. The feeling seems to be that "it's all very childish" or only appropriate when used with an intelligent group who are good at amateur dramatics.

Certainly, a drama club where presentations of a more formal kind are rehearsed and performed should have a significant place in the activities of most big hospitals and other institutions. However, drama along the lines already discussed has also an important contribution to make, which has until recently been neglected. The reasons for this neglect, I would suggest, are preconceived ideas about the nature of drama on the part of both staff and clients. One staff attitude is that drama has little relevance to the hard reality of living that must eventually be faced by many; by illustration I hope to show how drama can in fact help in adjusting to this reality. Similarly, adult clients often remark "I don't want to be an actor, so why have I been sent here?" Nevertheless the importance of drama within an overall adult therapeutic programme is fast gaining recognition.

The criticism that "drama is childish" is often justified because the choice of material has been inappropriate to the situation. I am not surprised when clients rebel at being asked to "be a balloon," particularly when they have never done drama before. For many, even leaving the security of their chair is a difficult task. I was hampered in one ward situation by the over-enthusiasm of a jolly nurse who, leading a very timid middle-aged woman into the group, said, "Come along Mrs Smith, I know you're going to enjoy yourself." Mrs Smith was far from certain that she was going to enjoy her first drama lesson and huddled in a chair concentrating on her knitting.

Chairs are often very safe places and there is no reason why they should not serve as a starting point. Most of the exercises for warming up the body, for using the voice and improvisation can be done in a seated group, though many sessions have not progressed beyond the halting play-reading.

To illustrate the above point: I was working with a new group in a short-stay psychiatric ward; they arrived feeling either apathetic or suspicious of what I might ask them to do. They all sat down and talked amongst themselves, so I sat with them and joined in the conversation, which was about the daily routine. The group began telling me how very bored they were − "there's only the radio." We began discussing radio plays and how they were made; it was then only a short step for the group to decide that we could make up our own play. They decided it was to be a Russian spy thriller − James Bond theme music provided the right atmosphere. We recorded the play on to a cassette tape-recorder and played it back at the end of the session. Apart from the change of attitude towards drama, in itself important, members of the group began to get up off their chairs spontaneously when various sound effects were needed in the play such as doors slamming or footsteps running down the corridor.

The above instance shows that a positive response can be obtained by using adult material, and, as with all groups, by "starting where the group is at."

With some adult groups I have found that calling the lesson "Relaxation" rather than "Drama" has meant less initial apprehension. The session can start with simple exercises such as tensing one limb at a time then letting it flop, working through the whole body from the feet upwards, or deep breathing exercises, inhaling and exhaling to a count of six. "Keep Fit," "Health and Beauty," "Relaxation" are often more acceptable terms than the rather nebulous "Movement." Start with simple breathing and body exercises, such as the relaxation already described, and progress to more adventurous work.

Drama can be of positive help to adults:

(i)   To counteract the effects of institutionalization (very important for clients in long-stay situations, in prisons, mental hospitals and centres for the subnormal). Remember that for people who have sat for perhaps many years it will be a slow, gradual process for them to feel confident enough to walk about, let alone do anything more energetic.

(ii)   As a medium for working through important situations which may have to be faced in the future, e.g. job interviews, wondering how the boss will react to one's previous record.

(iii)   As a situation for exploring attitudes, thoughts, feelings and ideas. Comparable to a group-therapy situation, but by using drama expression can be extended beyond just talking.

(iv)   As a means of expressing and understanding fantasy.

(v)   As a means of discovering identity, particularly by role-playing and role-training.

As with other age-groups, I would also draw attention to the enjoyment experienced through participatory creative drama, which in itself is therapeutic.

Guidelines

> Debates, quizzes, charades, panel games are all good starters.
>
> Use current news items from television/newspapers as improvisation starters.
>
> Encourage the group's own inventiveness into finding ways of overcoming strikes, reorganizing the Government, coping with housing problems (remember that the session may give some members the very first opportunity to "have their say").
>
> Improvise around conflict themes such as older/younger generation, staff/patient relationships.
>
> Use play-reading with plenty of flexibility in types of role. Allow people to experiment with roles far removed from themselves — this often leads into role-playing of personal situations.
>
> Victorian music-hall songs and party games make ideal starters with geriatric groups. Also, improvisation around "Now when I was a child. . . ." Do not impose "touching" exercises if the group or individual appear resistant — provide the opportunity for it to "happen or not" through improvisation and movement.

Adult groups often arrive at a session feeling suspicious —
if they ask "What's it for?" or "Why do we have to come?"
discuss it fully. Don't keep an air of mystery.

If you use a tape-recorder, ask the group and see how
they feel. If they want the tape wiped clean at the end,
respect this. Remember that the work will only develop
in any depth if the leader has the trust of the group; this
trust will not be possible if the session is abused for
finding out information.

Many adults, through involvement in drama, express
feelings to which they may never have admitted before,
especially in front of others. Allow plenty of time for
support and "caring" on these occasions (see especially
the "group rock" exercise described in Chapter 11 under
"Trust Exercises").

Practical Illustrations
1 The Remedial Drama Group were asked to visit a psychiatric
clinic in Brussels. It was obvious on arrival that the thirty white-
coated staff — doctors, nurses, physiotherapists, occupational
therapists, etc. — who were seated along one wall, notebooks in
hand, wanted a demonstration with a group of eight patients. I
pointed out that this was an experimental session and that I
would not allow an audience. There was a tense silence, until
the head psychiatrist slowly took off his shoes and removed his
tie — the rest of the staff followed his example!
    The session began with simple warm-up games, lots of fun
and laughter and frequent changing of partners, with staff and
patients mixing freely. As we progressed, more patients appeared
through the windows, some pyjama-clad, eager to know what
was going on. Within an hour the group had grown to
seventy!
    We had done mainly physical work so far, body exercises and
mime situations, and the group were resting curled up on the
floor. I suggested that we would improvise a journey: they could
go alone or with others and it was their choice where the journey
took them and what might happen on the way. While they were
resting I played some music with a great variety of mood, pace,

electronic and orchestral sound and, after a few moments, I suggested they begin their journey whenever they felt ready.

Some members of the group lay on the floor, eyes closed, and experienced their journey "dream" style; others moved towards an imagined source, shielding their eyes or turning away in fear as they were drawn nearer; small groups paddled boats and explored caverns with stalactites, climbed difficult mountains or crossed turbulent seas and rivers. There was a climax when at last everyone arrived at the end of their journey, then relaxed and enjoyed what they had found. It had been a very moving experience for most of the group and they enjoyed relaxing at the end and just thinking about what they had done before the session was concluded.

Afterwards one patient, a middle-aged woman who was chronically depressed and had been in hospital for several years, came to speak to me. Her eyes were shining and she seemed very peaceful as she told me that this was the first time since her depression that she had really "felt" anything; the journey for her was like a journey through her illness and had convinced her that there really was "light at the end of the tunnel." She felt very hopeful about the future. Her psychiatrist also said that he felt this was a real breakthrough and that jointly they would be able to build on it in her treatment.

After a lunch break, everyone wanted to continue. We began by experimenting with rhythms with parts of the body, on the floor and furniture. This developed into small group work around a central "Jungle" theme; each group made up their own ideas, made masks if they wanted, used records or composed chants and dances, invented a human totem pole and staged a sacrifice. We let each group show their idea and then linked them all together with a great happening at the end, involving everybody in dance and chants before it died right down into relaxation.

Half way through the activities a new patient arrived, in pyjamas, who had stayed in bed for weeks because he was not interested in anything. He said he wanted to help organize the programme and proved most imaginative, throwing in ideas and contributing to the final phase.

We relaxed for a long time at the end. It had been an extremely strenuous day, and one patient who suffered from severe insomnia went into a deep sleep.

This illustration is important as it shows:

(i)   That significant changes can happen even in a "once-only" session which can facilitate progress in other treatment.

(ii)   That it is possible to work effectively in a large group situation.

(iii) That new experiences were possible in relationships, especially in the staff/patient context (the staff in discussion said how difficult it had been to adjust to this — experiencing and sharing something with the patients and being less isolated from them).

2 I was working intensively with a large group of mixed sub-normal adults. The staff had been trying action methods for teaching simple things but said that the attempt had fizzled out. They also said that improvisation was not possible because the group thought it silly.

The group had been learning to tell the time, using a large cardboard block. This took on a new lease of life when we were able to make the clock tick by using the metronome at varying speeds and to make it chime the hours with a large cymbal. Stories about clocks followed and mimes of different types of clocks, building clocks with several people.

After a breather, I asked the group where they would like to go on an outing. The answer was "into town" so I said "Let's go" and we placed rows of chairs down the middle of the room to simulate a coach. It was at this point that several of the older men decided it was silly and opted out. However, the rest of us boarded the bus, bought tickets and sorted out the correct change. We became involved in a traffic jam, encountered policemen and traffic lights, singing favourite songs in between incidents. Then we got stuck on a hill and at this point the men who had opted out pushed the bus successfully to the top of the hill, whereupon we had a puncture. The men gave us a demonstration of how to change a wheel as well as a check-up on the engine.

When we arrived in town everyone wanted to go to a cafe. It was almost teatime anyway so we built it into the session with waitresses, orders, disputes over bills. We boarded the bus again, got lost and eventually arrived back at the hospital with a lusty sing-song.

Once this story had got under way even the most reluctant person was prepared to join in because he felt he had something "manly" to do. The staff found it very helpful that they could incorporate so many learning tasks into a theme which also gave scope for imaginative expression.

3 In a short-stay psychiatric unit we had been improvising around machine and computer themes. People made up noises, became operators on a conveyor belt and used partners to be different types of machine.

We went on to machine invention. Each group devised a machine never invented before. There was a great deal of laughter and whispering, then absorption from one group before they suddenly announced, "We are a machine for chopping up psychiatrists!" The other groups then wanted to join in the theme and suggested they had a conveyor belt system for remaking psychiatrists; they were chopped up, reprocessed in various ways and remodelled at the end. Everyone had the chance to either "design" a psychiatrist or act the part of the "ideal shrink." The whole group became involved to a high degree and were obviously expressing many "unacceptable" feelings through this improvisation.

The staff, who had joined in, said that it was most helpful in gaining insight into the group and seeing how they were perceived by the patients.

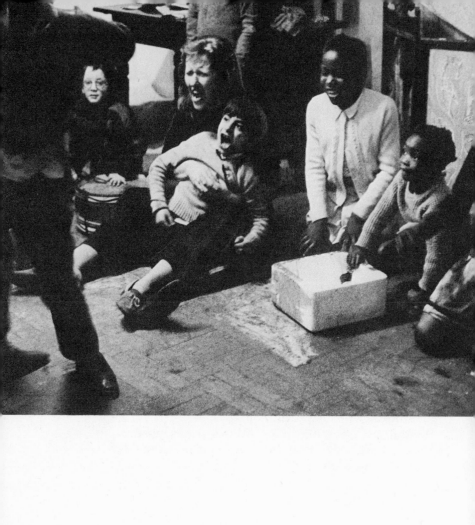

9 Frequent Difficulties

The most common distress call I receive is concerned with aggression and how to cope with it. Many staff feel that if they use drama with an aggressive group the anti-social behaviour will increase and may well get out of control, and this is often used as a reason for not doing drama.

It is a moot point as to whether the nature of man is basically aggressive. There is ample research to suggest that aggression is culturally conditioned, i.e. where competition is encouraged, self-assertion and a degree of aggression are necessary (anthropologists have found that where competitive behaviour is actively discouraged from an early age, aggressive behaviour is almost if not entirely absent). Therefore in our own society, which is basically competitive, we need not be surprised that aggressive qualities often break culturally imposed boundaries. It is unrealistic, too, to think that aggression will just disappear through sanctions, heavy tranquillizers or denial.

There are many situations involving feelings of aggression towards different types of authority that can be utilized successfully in the drama session. Very often a group needs the opportunity to "have their say." They are sometimes reluctant to do this because they are worried about the consequences. If properly handled, the drama session can provide the means not only for expressing pent-up frustrations but also for examining them; this could result in the child or adult realizing how much belongs to his fantasy notions of authority and how much he has legitimate cause to be angry. Some people are very afraid of their own aggressive feelings and the drama session can help them realize that their destructive fantasies cannot actually kill.

Verbal expression is not always the answer to the physical violence of a group; it is more effective to use physical means

73

to channel this. However, disaster will occur if the overall implications of the session are not considered in advance. At one psychiatric hospital where I ran a weekend workshop for nurses, occupational therapists and doctors there was great enthusiasm to start something in the ward. After I left, the patient group was told, "Now you can all be as angry and aggressive as you like." The results may be imagined; of course the staff panicked, having let the whole situation get totally out of control. I was summoned back to provide additional training on structure!

However aggressive we allow our group to be, the situation must have a flexible framework. Furthermore the group/individual must feel assured that if they lost control (as many are scared of doing) the leader will look after them. It is frequently disturbing, and working against reality, to place people in total freedom. But we must not confuse the use of frameworks with imposing sanctions. I would not use my own personal standards to impose moral boundaries on the group, but I must place a limit beyond which it would be self-destructive for the child or adult to go.

The leader should always build "control factors" into any drama programme. These are signals or cues whereby the group can stop or change tempo without cutting across the established activity. For example, the simple instruction "Freeze" is more constructive than a command to stop. The "freeze" can be justified within the context of a session — an action-replay photograph or a sudden police swoop to search for drugs, arms or an escaped prisoner. I was working in a hospital with a group of subnormal boys who got involved in a cowboy improvisation which became very noisy and out of control. In desperation I came in as the sheriff and shot them all down. They all lay motionless on the floor and eventually one of them whispered, "Go on, bury us then." Having interred them all, the same child hissed "You've not said the prayers," and I had to switch roles to vicar and say the appropriate things over each grave. I did not have to envisage where the improvisation would lead because the group all got up and became ghosts to haunt the dreams of the wicked sheriff. Not only was a natural control factor used effectively but the pace of the session slowed down without destroying the continuity.

Movement improvisation which includes simulated fights can be equally satisfying when done in slow motion. If the group needs an additional stimulus use examples of popular films, commercials, sports programmes which all use slow-motion techniques. Certain records such as James Bond theme music and popular cowboy music reproduce extremely well at a slower speed. I have sometimes used music at the normal speed and then slowed it down — without any instruction from me, the group automatically went into slow motion when the tempo changed.

Drums and tambours can be helpful as control factors, especially when the actions of say a stylized fight are done to a regular rhythm. The leader can then change the tempo, getting faster or slower when appropriate.

I must recount one instance where the drum control factor proved ineffective. I was working on a training programme specifically dealing with aggression; the students were ninety per cent nuns in full habit, the remainder priests in jeans and sweaters. We had worked around fight practices both unarmed and with imaginary swords, cutlasses and guns. I wanted to illustrate a more developed improvisation and we chose the theme of an occupied city. They divided into two groups, one being the occupying army and the other the local inhabitants who built a barricade across the room to suggest a "no-go area." The army were patrolling on one side while the people were making clandestine missiles ready for a surprise attack. I had made the point at the beginning of the session that the barrier was impenetrable. A dawn raid took place which became more and more violent as the drum beats got louder, but initially there was no noise. To overcome their shyness I suggested that they mouthed their insults "as if the sound had been turned down on the television"; I said that I would gradually turn the sound up so that I could first of all hear them in the distance and then slowly louder and louder. The groups became so involved in the situation that when I "turned up full volume" the noise was completely deafening and drowned the noise of my drum, which meant that it could no longer be used as an effective control factor! Fortunately the percussion cupboard was near and I was able to change to an enormous bass drum which penetrated through the din.

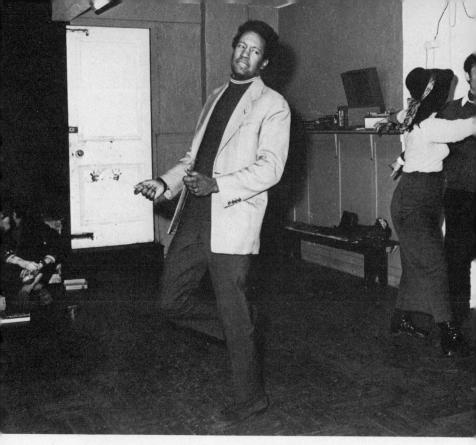

A similar situation which just did not work was when one child overturned a tea-chest full of milk-bottle tops. My suggestion, that we should all be park-keepers clearing up for a Ministry inspection, went totally unheeded and the whole group had a glorious fight, hurling milk-bottle tops at each other and at me!

Many stories such as "The Adventure of Oseo" (see Chapter 2) have ready-made control factors, and these are very effective with aggressive groups.

In the previous chapters I have tried not to idealize the practical working situations for the various drama sessions described. However, I know that individual readers will have specific problems in their own environments which can make it very difficult even to consider doing drama. I have experienced many of these myself and will attempt to describe how I overcame some of them, not always satisfactorily!

In the traditional school, space for doing drama is always at a premium. Too often the school hall, as well as being vast and thereby encouraging children to rush from one end to the other, is situated as a central thoroughfare with the classrooms leading off it. Frequently it has to double up for radio and television programmes, as a library or gymnasium, for assembly and school dinners. Furthermore it is used intermittently for indoor games in wet weather, special talks and other untimetabled activities, which can be very disheartening when planning a long-term programme.

In the multi-purpose hall it is always disturbing, having gained the concentration of the group, to have a sudden interruption. This can sometimes be a well-meaning school secretary looking for somebody, but the mere fact of her coming into the room and saying "Oh, I'm sorry," and then retreating can disrupt a whole session. Unlike other lessons it is not easy to "switch off" the drama while coping with interruptions or even discrete signals. Additionally the drama session is often a source of great curiosity to other classes who will seize any opportunity to press their noses up against the windows or deliberately walk through the hall en route to the lavatory/office/stock cupboard.

In the large school hall I find it best to section off a working area either with screens, rostra or chairs and I often do this with the group at the beginning of a session. The rest of the space can be utilized as "the space beyond," for example unknown territory that has to be explored, conquered or navigated. With one group we had a small working area at the opposite end of the stage; the large space between became a minefield they had to cross to escape from a prison camp and the stage was the country of safety to which they were travelling. This way the entire space was used, but in sections.

I use gymnastic equipment — wall-bars, ropes, climbing-nets — to build exciting environments such as jungles, mountains, ships' rigging, difficult journeys or factory machinery.

When the hall is being used as a thoroughfare by individuals or whole classes the best solution is to incorporate these interruptions into the session — a busy market place, a railway station, in fact any place where there is busy activity. With the interrupter who comes in with a message it is more difficult, and one headmistress looked askance when, as she hurried in to see me, I turned to the group and said "The King's messenger has made it at last!" Sometimes a simple injunction to the group — "Freeze

like statues." — can help, but usually I find the only way is to
have a diplomatic talk to the staff explaining how disruptive
such an interruption can be. The sound effects of dinner ladies
setting up tables, chairs and cutlery can be incorporated into
the session.

In many schools the drama lesson has to be confined to the
classroom. This can be a strain through lack of space and also
because it is usually not possible to make a noise. Although
these are severe limitations they do not preclude doing drama
at all. I rearranged my classroom so that the tables and chairs
were "in the round," which left a small working space in the
centre (of course if there was time and we did not want to make
use of the furniture we stacked it away). Many exercises can be
done in a confined space and in fact can help children to cope
with cramped conditions. For more energetic activities I often
divide the class in two and let each have a turn of using the space
while the others are more static.

Not being able to make a noise is more difficult to cope with
and there is a limit to how long a quiet drama class can last.
Obviously we can try developing all the movement and quiet-
talking aspects but this can prove very one-sided. I found that I
could often slot in a drama lesson when the next-door classes
were elsewhere, on the games field or watching a television
programme. In addition, in fine weather, I would use the playground or games field, which proved very successful. In secondary
schools I gained the sympathy of the domestic science and
chemistry departments and utilized room in the laboratories.

In some schools I have been asked to use drama with individual
children and small groups selected from different classes, only to
find that there was no space available. Although far from ideal
we were able to use the potential of the cloakroom — good for
improvising bus and train journeys. I sometimes ended up taking
individual children in the school stock cupboard. Despite a notice
on the door I was constantly interrupted by Miss Smith wanting
sugar paper *but* the small space definitely proved an advantage,
not only for the timid, withdrawn child but also for containing
some of the aggressive children.

Newly-designed schools also have their problems. Much of the
equipment and paintwork is "too nice to be touched," in complete
contrast to the more homely, though rough and ready, atmosphere

of some of our older schools. Frequently the amount of glass in new schools prevents any real privacy and drama does sometimes need to be very private. Again, I have used passers-by peering in around the theme of zoos. Luckily some of these large halls do have curtains or blinds.

Many of the physical problems in hospitals are similar to those described in schools and leaders can adapt the various ways of handling these to their own situations. One difficulty that I have found nerve-racking in a hospital is that of patients being constantly called out of the session to see the doctor or visitors. This would happen no matter which day we had drama and there was a limit to my invention for when it came to incorporating these interruptions in the drama session. I found the only solution was to have knowledge in advance of who would have to leave and to gain the co-operation of the nursing attendant who, instead of calling the person from the doorway, would come in quietly without knocking and speak directly to the person concerned without having to ask my permission.

Hospital screens are invaluable for chopping up vast wards into more manageable working areas.

When the only space available is a multi-purpose recreation room, there is naturally resentment towards a drama group which intrudes into other activities such as table tennis, cards or private conversation. I started by making drama an unobtrusive activity in one corner, beginning with play-reading or discussion, and found that many of the other people became so intrigued that they wanted to join us. Occasionally, if we were improvising, we asked the other groups if they would carry on with their activities but within the context of our "play" — card games and billiards in a Western saloon bar, people chatting in a Doctor's waiting room. More often than not this worked and not only gave the drama group more scope but also incorporated people who had hitherto been very resistant. The crucial factor was, I think, that they were not being asked to do something different, which of course brings us back to that most fundamental point, "starting where the group are at."

10 Psychodrama and Role-playing

There is a great deal of misunderstanding about psychodrama, and many leaders feel they have to call their drama-in-hospitals, or even music and movement, "psychodrama" in order to validate it. It seems part of the current trend of putting the words "psycho" in front of, or "therapy" after, activities done in mental hospitals. This should logically give us psycho-geranium growing!

However, without wishing to diminish the importance of psychodrama, I would suggest that it has a far more limited application than the wide scope of remedial drama as part of a therapeutic programme, with which this book is concerned.

Psychodrama is a term used first by Moreno in America in the 1920s to describe a specialized form of psychotherapy in which the patient enacts his conflicts rather than talking about them. It should *only* be used under the advice of a psychiatrist or by those who have followed prescribed psychodrama training. It is irresponsible to attempt psychodrama with only superficial knowledge as it can produce a dynamic situation where defences are low and suggestibility very high. The inherent dangers are obvious and to be compared with those resulting from amateur psychotherapy. Furthermore, since psychodrama belongs to what is termed "in-depth" treatment, its use is inappropriate in situations that most leaders have to face.

However, having clarified this point, I would go on to say that there are many techniques developed through psychodrama which can be incorporated, with care, into remedial situations — just as many modern psychodramatists are now making use of a broader range of creative techniques and action methods.

The leader must be aware of other treatment that the client may be undergoing. It would be confusing for all concerned, if a client is attending child guidance as well as remedial drama, if the leader was unaware that the therapist at the clinic wanted a critical issue left alone. Conversely, exploration in the drama session may well facilitate progress at the clinic and it is important that all staff liaise.

The opportunity for using psychodrama techniques will often occur spontaneously or develop from a creative drama situation, usually when there has been a shift in emphasis from group experience to an individual's personal problem. Similarly, an evocative piece of music, an atmosphere or a scene in a play may give someone the wish to explore further his personal feelings. It can happen quite suddenly and the leader must watch out for this. For example, if a client bursts into tears without warning the leader can ask him if there is anything the group can do to help. The client must understand that he is not being pressurized to explore a situation and often the support and acceptance of the rest of the group is sufficient in itself (see Trust Exercises in Chapter 11). Remember, too, that the person in question may not have access to supportive help away from the session. Always allow plenty of time for recovery if someone has become very distressed.

The term sociodrama is applied to the exploration of a *group's* feelings and problems rather than those of an individual. The techniques are comparable to psychodrama techniques — for example role-reversing two sections of the community, perhaps tenants and housing authorities. However, I have already mentioned the use of "social" drama under other headings and it needs no further elaboration here.

USEFUL PSYCHODRAMA TECHNIQUES

1. Role-playing: as its name implies this gives a person the chance to play himself and to gain insight through the group's interaction and empathy. It also provides opportunities for trying out "new roles" in a safe situation.

2. Role-reversal: this is where the client plays the part of a parent/magistrate/teacher with whom he may be in conflict, while somebody else in the group plays him. This leads to insight into both sides of the conflict and understanding of how the "other person" might feel.

3. Doubling: this is where somebody in the group speaks on behalf of somebody else who is having difficulty in verbal communication. The double speaks in the first person as if he is the voice of the other.

4. Empty chair: this can be used as another character in a "drama." This often facilitates deeper involvement where confrontation is concerned. There is less embarrassment in confronting an imaginary person sitting on a chair than in speaking to an actual person face to face.

Practical Illustration
A group of ten immigrant children aged 8 and 9 referred for "aggression."

We were involved in an improvisation on cowboys and Indians when a fight started for real between two boys. I physically parted them and one of them turned on me and said, "It's against the law to touch me — I'm going to get my Mum from the factory, she'll come and sort you out." He was already half way to the door; I pointed out that he was legally under my care until the end of the afternoon but that he could go and fetch his Mum at four o'clock if he wanted and I would wait for them. He seemed satisfied at this, after some deliberation, and I asked him what he would say to his Mum when he found her: "Why don't you show us?"

We used the rostra to make a small drama room where I sat and waited, while he chose a friend to play his Mum and went off to fetch her from the factory. He brought her back and thundered on the door. I then suggested that he played his mother; he portrayed an enormous overpowering woman who was more concerned with stating her rights than with protecting her son. We role-reversed again and I played his mother while he played me. The situation literally played itself out. The boy became in subsequent sessions a far more integrated member of the group.

11 Further Practical Suggestions

This chapter, in conjunction with Chapter 2, will provide a wide range of material from which the reader may draw and adapt to his own work situation. It includes work which overlaps into other media such as art and music.

Although many of these ideas will seem just like "exercises," they can be developed and incorporated into overall projects. The categories are very flexible.

MASKS AND MAKE-UP

Masks and make-up are useful aids to creative drama but care should be taken in their handling. Always allow enough time for the process of removing masks and returning to the here and now. Many people become very involved in their mask role and sudden stopping can be destructive.

Masks have been criticized for provoking aggressive behaviour; it would be fairer to say that the wearing of a mask sometimes gives a person another identity through which he feels safe to express the less "acceptable" sides of himself.

Make-up has certain advantages in that mobility of expression is still possible and there is a great variety of facial designs. On the other hand, masks usually provide a safer insulation in that the person feels less exposed.

N.B. It is important for masks to be comfortable. They should not make people feel that they cannot breathe or that they cannot see where they are going because the eyeholes are too small.

Hints on mask-making
1. Newspaper and sticky-tape make quick once-only masks.

2. Masks from toy shops make ideal bases for building more elaborate masks.

3. Large pieces of expanded polystyrene (used in packing — can be obtained free from TV shops, etc.) can be cut, melted or sculpted and then painted — very light and comfortable to wear.

4. Chicken-wire and papier mâché makes a good mask base — half masks, i.e. not covering mouth, are often more comfortable.

5. Use boxes as bases for masks, to be cut, added to or painted.

Make-up

1. Make sure the group are wearing old clothes/overalls — collars are particularly prone to get grubby.

2. Leichner grease paint sticks are most ideal — a wide variety of colours including gold and silver, also liquid blue, gold, brown body paint.

3. Have ample supplies of tissues or toilet paper, cleansing cream/ liquid paraffin for removal. Soap and water usually removes body liquid.

4. Check up on whether any members have allergies or sensitive skins.

5. Always make sure face is covered in thin layer of cream or liquid paraffin before applying make-up.

Ideas for Trying out

(a)   Experimental session using make-up allowing group just to try out ideas both on themselves and each other. Have plenty of mirrors. Do not hurry this.

(b)   From ideas created in *(a)* develop into themes/stories.

(c)   Experiment with blacking-out faces — black greasepaint or burnt cork; let black children use white make-up. Develop an improvisation.

(d)   Experiment with make-up under different-coloured lights to stimulate imagination and develop atmosphere (include ultra-violet lighting).

(e)   Mask-making session — using wide variety of materials, let group make whatever masks they like; may take one to two sessions. Finished masks can be used in an improvisation.

(f)   As above but contructing masks round specific theme.

(g)   Give ten minutes to make a mask out of newspaper and sticky-tape — improvise (mirrors essential).

(h) Combine masks and make-up to give two groups their own identity, e.g. "The Space Men and the Cobweb People."

(i) Brown paper bags with eyes and mouth cut out — use as neutral face for person to build up new character.

(j) Do not neglect highly stylized mask and make-up use in pageants/Mardi Gras.

(k) Try out whole body masks, e.g. a sack with eyes cut out, large cardboard boxes with eye and arm-holes; can be developed into human puppets.

DRESSING-UP

Dressing-up is popular with all age-groups but can sometimes blunt creative imagination by the clothes being too inflexible,

difficult to wear, or too nice to mess up. Keep clothes as simple
and as adaptable as possible and renew at intervals. A weekly
trip to the launderette incorporated into the project takes care
of grubbiness!

(a)   Large box assorted hats (jumble sales!) — let each person
choose hat and play character it suggests. Develop into pairs
and group work.
(b)   Use long lengths of sheeting/butter muslin/chiffon as veils,
trains, ghosts.
(c)   Free improvisation with large pieces of sheeting, individually
and in groups.
(d)   Circular wrap-over skirts can also be used for improvising
— toreadors, all types of cloak.
(e)   Large box of heterogeneous clothes and props with plenty
of nice ones as well as rough ones.
(f)   Fashion parades, seriously and in fun — use newspaper,
crepe paper, large pieces of material to make fifteen-minute
costumes.
(g)   Utilize cardboard boxes and corrugated paper for improvising other forms of dressing-up — Martians, zombies, Egyptian
mummies, imaginary monsters.

PAINTING AND MODELLING
I do not propose to enumerate exhaustively the visual art methods
already used in many schools. However, by a few illustrations it
should be obvious how these could be used in conjunction with
other creative media. We already have overlap between disciplines
in mask-making and decorating, since these of course include
painting and modelling.
　　Visual art can be used both as a stimulus for dramatization
and as a means of developing an improvised theme. It can also
be built into the overall drama structure. I have often used
painting as an "arrival" activity while people are coming in ones
and twos and settling down.

Useful Materials
1. Large quantities of powder paints — try mixing with detergent
to get thick consistency.
2. Large range of brushes including six-inch distemper brushes.

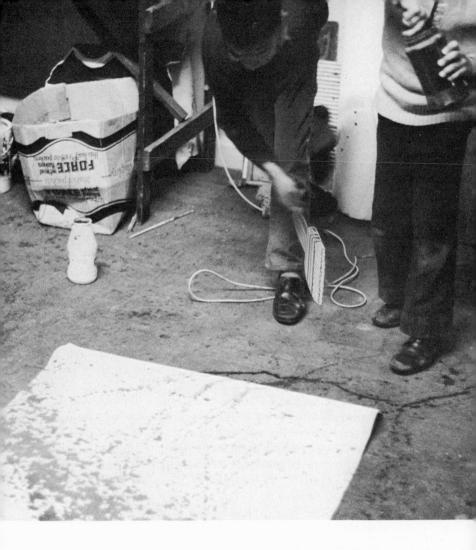

3. Inexhaustible supply of "junk" — small/large boxes, straws, raffia, polystyrene, collage materials, tissue paper, textured and coloured material, foam rubber, corrugated, cardboard tubes, wood shavings, foil, newspaper, wire, bottle tops.
4. Paper clips, rubber bands, elastic, string, stapler, glue (jars are better than tubes; the latter can get trodden on), stronger glue for cardboard, sticky-tape, insulating tape.
5. Chicken-wire, extra large boxes for strong bases for models and sculptures.
6. Thick felt tips, chalks.

7. Modelling clay, and play pastry (flour, water and salt; colour the flour with powder paint before adding water).
8. Aerosol paintsprays.

Ideas for Trying out
(a)   Use coloured pastry to develop touch and manipulation before making actual "things"; kneading, rolling, pressing, flattening, thumping, coiling can be done to music or singing games.
(b)   Try drawing/painting in different dimensions — let group chalk on floor. Could be developed into improvisation — "pavement artist" — or whole group could draw fishes, sea-weed, etc., for underwater theme. (Many children are happier painting pictures lying on their tummies.)
(c)   Use large boxes to build environment for improvisation — glue together and cover with newspaper and paint. Corrugated cardboard covered in straw (glass packing) makes good huts.
(d)   As well as building up from the floor, suspend down from the ceiling — clouds, raffia and string to make creepy forest/maze/cobweb.
N.B. If the ceiling is too high make a false ceiling by screw hooks in walls and strong string criss-crossed across the room — can then be used for suspending.
(e)   Build large statues/models to stimulate improvisation — for example, one of my groups built a ten-foot totem pole out of boxes and polystyrene; several children were able to work on it at the same time using a stepladder and *buckets* of paint. They named the totem pole Jo-jonjon and chanted his name as they danced round him — this led into mud-hut building and a complete story around hunting, fighting and village life. (Incidentally, it was interesting that two of the most violent boys, having built their hut and put a skull and crossbones outside, were then absorbed for twenty minutes using it as a Wendy house and playing at tea-parties.)
(f)   Cover wall or floor with *large* pieces of paper (large tear-off rolls are now available) for finger painting, hand and foot painting and collages around themes. Distemper brushes tied on to broomsticks are useful for extending scope.
(g)   Chicken-wire bases/papier mâché for making helmets, both modern and historical.

(h) Bottle tops, rings off canned drinks, stuck on to card/
material (hessian or sheeting) and sprayed with silver/gold
aerosol for making armour, robots and space monsters.

(i) Papier mâché, beans, coiled coarse string — sprayed gold
and silver — for jewellery, treasure, crowns.

(j) Use papier mâché/yogurt pots for making hand puppets,
maracas.

(k) Paint faces/eyes on hands, fingers or feet for puppet work.

(l) Tear up newspapers for confetti, snowstorms.

PHOTOGRAPHY

Despite its important role in society, from holiday snaps to live
pictures from the moon, photography is still a somewhat
neglected medium in the context of education and therapy.
Photography is a visual language and can be applied in many
ways to drama. Not only do photographs and film provide an
effective stimulus, but the actual taking of photographs during
a session by members of the group, the leader or an assistant
can add an important dimension. In the past, photographers
attending a session have been considered intruders or disrupters
of something very personal and private. This is obviously the
case when a photographer, a stranger to the group, is imported
from outside for a single visit. However, I have experimented
with integrating a photographer assistant into a group from the
beginning and found that his presence in fact added to the
potential of the group.

Although "photographic therapy" is very much in its infancy
I have already observed several distinct advantages:

(i) The leader has a permanent visual record of the group.

(ii) Through habituation the group are not camera-shy and
therefore do not "pose."

(iii) The role of the photographer can be integrated into many
themes — news programmes, journalism.

(iv) Members of the group, particularly the verbally backward,
are given an opportunity to develop a new creative medium — I
find that a poor linguist is often advanced in "visual" communication (this of course also applies to painting and modelling).

(v) As with mirrors, a person is able to see himself.

(vi) Provides a new learning skill which can motivate even the most uninterested.

(vii) Encourages observation, accuracy, intuition and imagination.

Equipment need not be complex or expensive. Polaroid cameras are fairly cheap and are useful because they provide instant feedback, but the films are rather expensive. Black and white negative film for "orthodox" cameras is relatively cheap to buy and process (some groups may try developing their own).

Obviously, few leaders will have the good fortune to be able to command the assistance of a professional photographer; however, a helper willing to supervise those children experimenting in the medium, and to try it himself, should prove satisfactory.

(*a*)   Use colour slides and film to stimulate improvisations and to provoke discussion rather than passive entertainment. (See Appendix I for useful films in this context.)

(*b*)   Send group out with cameras to record things that interest them.

(*c*)   Develop a visual documentary around a current topic.

(*d*)   Use photography to bring a contemporary dimension to historical stories. Similarly, old-established topics can be revitalized by using new media.

(*e*)   Use the role of photographer in reportage, sports coverage, news scoops, police photographer, fashion.

(*f*)   Use experimentally for abstract ideas in texture, collage, etc.

(*g*)   Important "evidence" in criminal trial, surgical operations.

PUPPETS

Glove and finger puppets, as well as being important in themselves, also lead to other activities. Very often people will speak through a puppet when they feel unable to speak themselves.

Make sure that glove puppets are not too heavy for very small fingers to support.

(*a*)   Use hands and fingers without puppets to "talk," express moods, fight.

(*b*)   As above but paint eyes, faces, etc., on fingers or palms.

(*c*)   Use highly differentiated finger puppets for playing out family situations.

(*d*)   A piece of sheet draped over chairs provides a screen over which the puppets can appear.

(*e*)   Make sure puppets are strong enough to survive a lot of fighting and aggression.

(*f*)   Encourage the group to improvise their own themes around puppet characters.

(*g*)   Use old socks and gloves for making quick puppets.

(*h*)   A sheet with a light behind provides a means of developing shadow puppets — the cut-out variety which are held against the screen (use old X-ray films as an alternative to stiff card). Shapes and figures can also be made with the hands and the whole body. The latter can be developed in many ways by distorting shadows, or by several people forming one shadow — a six-armed goddess. The muted lighting facilitates confidence.

MUSIC AND SINGING

It is not necessary to be a professional musician to make use of music creatively, though if the help of music staff and others who play instruments can be enlisted so much the better. Music on tapes and records will be the most frequently used, but live music such as a guitar will greatly enhance the session. Live piano music is less useful unless there is an extra person to play, because the leader cannot easily see his group, nor can he move among them. A guitarist can sit with the group and provide accompaniment for camp fire singing, Wild West themes, strolling minstrels, singing rounds and many other songs.

If a robust session is anticipated, avoid finely-tuned delicate instruments. Nothing is more infuriating to a music teacher than to find bent cymbals or out-of-tune chimes.

Useful instruments

1. Small and large drums.
2. Sleigh bells.
3. Chime bars.
4. Large tambour.
5. Large and small cymbals.
6. Tambourines.
7. Swanee whistles.
8. Woodblocks.
9. Wooden clackers and rattles.

Making musical instruments

Most of these instruments can be made by the group themselves. The finished product is more pleasing if covered in PVC or sprayed with aerosol.

1. Yoghurt pots, detergent bottles filled with rice, peas, macaroni, buttons.
2. Bottle-tops threaded on to wire hoops.
3. Strong rubber bands round wood frame.
4. Cake tins/catering-size vegetable tins — a layer of felt inside lid reduces tinny noise, alternatively cover in fablon or stretch inner tubing across.
5. Petrol drums and dustbin lids.

Hints on Choosing Music

1. Choose music with a specific purpose in mind when it is to
be used for a definite activity, e.g. relaxation or warm-up. Many
ballads and folk songs induce relaxation; rhythmic warm-up
music must not be too fast or too slow!

2. Always listen to improvisation music before using it with the
group BUT let the group formulate their own ideas.

N.B. Some electronic and similar music can have a very disturbing
effect on certain people — not necessarily the disturbed. If in
doubt ask advice.

3. Theme music should again be chosen specifically — film and
television themes, Wild West music.

Choice of music is a personal matter for the leader, but I
include a general list of records that I have found particularly
useful. It is by no means exhaustive and an afternoon spent in
a sympathetic record shop can yield many finds.

Relaxation:
1. "A Whiter Shade of Pale" (orchestral version)
2. "Blowin' in the Wind" (Peter Paul and Mary)

Warm-up:
1. "Tijuana Play the Beatles" (Music for Pleasure)
2. "Tijuana Sound of Brass" (Music for Pleasure)
3. "Swinging Safari" (Music for Pleasure)
4. "Listen, Move and Dance" (Vols. 1 and 2, EMI)

Improvisation:
1. "The World of TV Themes" (Decca)
2. "Listen, Move and Dance" (Vols. 3 and 4, EMI)
3. "Music from the Greek Islands" (Music for Pleasure)
4. "Negro Spiritual Songs for Children" (Music for Pleasure)
5. "Flute of Latin America"
6. "America Calls Africa Answers"
7. "Fingal's Cave" (Mendelssohn)
8. "The Planets Suite" (Holst)
9. "Peer Gynt Suite" (Grieg)
10. "Pictures at an Exhibition" (Moussorgsky)
11. "Façade Suite" (William Walton)

   12. Cowboy albums (Music for Pleasure and Decca)
   13. Volumes of film themes — including "silent" films
   14. Individual titles by Leroy Anderson
   15. Reggae titles
   16. Brass band music, circus marches, fairground music
   17. Programme music published by BBC Sound Archives; also
      volumes on Africa, etc.

(a)   Play a record for the group to paint to — group or individual
painting. The pictures can then be used for improvising.
(b)   Let part of group experiment with providing live music for
others to work to (can range from simple rhythms to full scale
sound effects). Incidentally, this is a good way of coping with
large numbers in a small place.
(c)   Experiment with sound effects without using actual
instruments — radiators, door handles, chair seats, etc.
(d)   Try getting the group to tape a series of sound effects,
then use for dramatic work.
(e)   Use natural rhythms such as heartbeats, walking, running,
taps dripping, to develop and reinforce rhythmic "sense," co-
ordination and later cross-rhythms and syncopations.
(f)   Let the group sit in pairs with foreheads, cheeks or necks
together, and hum, to feel sound vibrations — the sound produced
is reminiscent of music of the spheres and could be taped
and used.
(g)   Use very fast beats on a large cymbal for the following
exercise:
Starting crouched on the floor, "grow" up and out as the sound
increases until it reaches the climax, slowly sink into relaxation
again as vibrations die away — possibly suggest shouting on the
climax.
(h)   Use cymbal for clock striking, gongs.
(i)   Use metronome at different speeds for extending rhythmic
sense — can be used for movement exercises and also as stimulus
for ticking clocks, time bombs.
(j)   Use tambour for establishing and controlling pace of a
session.
(k)   Use pairs of bongo drums in one-to-one sessions for developing communication, i.e. question and answer "talked" on the
drums.

(l)   Make full use of action songs, singing games. Encourage group to compose their own to well-known tunes.

(m)   Songs from old-time music hall and sea shanties are very popular with adult groups.

(n)   Singing rounds.

MOVEMENT AND MIME

(a)   With a newly assembled group, suggest they all greet each person without using words. (Variations: say hello to everyone in the group, exchange names with everyone in the group.)

(b)   Let the group be on the floor and imagine themselves encased in a cocoon or tied up with rope — slowly, by exerting tremendous physical pressure, they burst through. (Use drum to build up exercise.)

(c)   Warm-up by vigorously rubbing all the muscles to lively music. Start with calves, thighs, tummies and work all the way up the body.

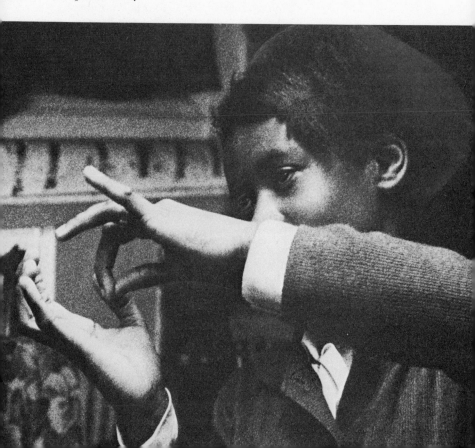

(d) Make use of a stylized "rehearsal" or preparation for concert, opera, ballet, Olympic Games or Space Mission as a means of loosening up the voice and body.

(e) Move large pieces of furniture through small spaces.

(f) Handle small, highly differentiated objects — class or partner guess what they are.

(g) Pass a ruler or screwed-up newspaper round the group using it as different objects (alternatively leave object in centre and group use it when ideas occur). Variation: pass imaginary lump of clay round circle and let each person model something.

(h) Walk through leaves . . . sand . . . treacle . . . hot cinders . . . with bare feet.

(i) Let half the group be heaps of metal, the other half inventors.

(j) In pairs, one person looking in mirror, the other *is* the mirror; change round. (Can be used as fun exercise with adult groups — let all women mime shaving and all men putting on false eyelashes.)

(k) Jump as high as possible as if pushing the floor away; jump as if the floor is pulling you down.

(l) Blow up imaginary balloons and burst them; blow up another person.

(m) Using one limb, move it like a piece of machinery; add a second limb — build up contrasting rhythms and shapes.

(n) In groups: "Be a Christmas card," then "Let all the characters come to life and improvise a story" (with or without words).

TRUST EXERCISES

Use these exercises with care according to the age and mood of the group. They are usually more appropriate with adult groups and are very effective for inducing calm and group communications, particularly after strong stimulus or possible distress.

(a) In pairs: one person sits on the floor, eyes closed, the other leads him round the room for a walk or to explore objects and textures. "Blind" person, before opening eyes, tells partner what it was like — did he feel safe or scared? Partners change round.

(b) In pairs: one person standing behind the other; person in front falls backwards with knees and hips straight and is caught by partner.

N.B. Pairs should work close together initially and gradually increase distance of "fall."

(*c*)   In fours, two people make a back, i.e. bend forward, hands on knees; third person stands between "backs" and falls forward on to one and back on to the other. Fourth person steadies faller — backs should give slightly as person falls.

(*d*)   One person in centre of closely knit circle, closes eyes and falls in any direction keeping body straight and is caught and pushed back; develop into a continuous process.

(*e*)   Two people stand facing, a few inches apart; hold hands and slowly lean back until arms are straight — each is supporting the other.

(*f*)   "Think of as many ways to balance your partner as possible."

(*g*)   Let one person be held horizontal on the shoulders of the group and rocked gently, perhaps to soft singing (a very reassuring exercise if a member has become distressed).

AGGRESSION EXERCISES

(*a*)   Face your partner, hands on each other's shoulders, try to push each other across the room.

(*b*)   Holding hands pull partner across the room — no jerking.

(*c*)   Shadow-box — with imaginary partner.

(*d*)   Fight imaginary partner using elbows/knees/feet.

(*e*)   Fight/box real partner, but no touching.

(f) Fencing duel using imaginary foils/broadswords/cutlasses — remind pairs to keep distance of two sword-lengths.

(g) Robin Hood fight on narrow bridge using broomsticks as staffs.

(h) "Made-up" swear words — start in a whisper, get louder and louder until shouting gradually dies down again.

(i) In pairs have shouted conversations just using "Ah" and "Oh."

(j) Have an "aggression corner" where things can be destroyed — paper for tearing, plastic bottles for jumping on, old pottery for hammering.

DANCE

(a) Use current popular dance and music, improvised initially — develop into choreographed sequences.

(b) Folk dances from other countries — Indian and Greek particularly useful and simple to learn.

(c) "Display" dances — can-can, kicking routine, slinky blues.

(d) Compose a dance round a particular theme — the seasons, War and Peace, the computer factory.

(e) Many "primitive" dances, warlike or festive can be learnt to simple drumming; use accurate film/video tape for instruction.

(f) Morris dances, sword dances and others less known from European cultures; Spanish dancing is excellent for releasing tension.

VOCAL GAMES

(a) Communicate in a "made-up" language.

(b) Have conversation with partner using numbers 1-100 or letters of alphabet.

(c) Let conversation start in whispers and become louder.

(d) Tongue-twisters.

(e) Converse in pairs using only "You must" and "I can't."

THEMES FOR IMPROVISATION AND PROJECTS
(a) A day in the life of our school.
(b) Machinery and factories.
(c) Road safety/first aid/using the telephone.
(d) Going into/leaving hospital, prison, school, home.
(e) The new arrival — baby, parent, grandparent, neighbours.
(f) Epics from history — Roman invasion, Battle of Waterloo,
Crimean War, the Titanic disaster; discovering America, India,
Australia.
(g) Current epics — the space age, famine, revolution, inventions, pollution, 1984.
(h) Social learning — Citizens' Advice Bureau, the Rent
Tribunal, Claimants' Union, magistrates' court, Police.
(i) Social problems — illegitimacy, drugs, racialism, homelessness, mental handicap and illness, urbanization, overcrowding,
human guinea-pigs.
(j) Themes from books, TV, films.
(k) Inventions — let group invent original machines.

STORYTELLING
(a) Well-known stories to be acted rather than read.
(b) The same material improvising different endings.
(c) Bible stories.
(d) Stories from other religions — the Ramayana, the Koran,
etc.
(e) Myth, folklore and legend from other countries and
civilizations, past and present.
(f) History and geography themes done in story form — the
life of a person/family during the Plague, the Crusades, the
Peasants' Revolt.
(g) Improvised stories in groups round a given title: "The
Haunted House," "I was a First Offender"; or give opening line
of story: "Many years ago, before engines and motor cars . . .";
"Preparation for my first space expedition to Mars was a long
and tedious business, but now launching is only a week away. . . ."
(h) Improvise stories from people's dreams.
(i) Read a story while the group dance it and supply sound
effects.

POETRY AND CHORAL SPEAKING
Utilizing the written word has many advantages, particularly
when working with adult groups. Quiet poetry-reading sessions,
where people can select their own likes from old and contemporary
work, are often ideal starting points. Writing one's own poetry
is sometimes just a stage further on from reading somebody else's.

Choral speaking, where the group is subdivided into voice pitch
and suitable material is read in unison, can be compared to a choir
singing the different parts of a score. I have found that individuals
who were unable to speak on their own gained confidence through
speaking with a group. Choral speaking provides the means of
developing a wide range of vocal power and dexterity and also
benefits general health through breathing exercises. It is an
intensely satisfying creative activity and also provides a medium
for exploring the potential of the group's combined resources.
Suitable material is suggested in Appendix II.

(a)   Have a poetry session around a particular theme with
members of the group selecting their own contributions.
(b)   Sometimes a person can identify with a particular mood
in a poem that he has not been able to crystallize before. This
could then be developed into re-enactment of this mood and
associated events.
(c)   Tape-recording verse-speaking helps to reinforce identity
and develop confidence; it is also useful for improvising new
poems when writing would be too laborious. (I have also used a
typewriter for recording poems as these are being composed.)
(d)   Use choral speaking both as a vocal presentation and with
movement, gesture or full dramatization.

PLAYS
The well-made play is often what is expected when people come
to a drama class for the first time. Rather than being purely an
end in itself the play can be developed in many other ways.

(a)   Use scripts with a wide range of age and character.
(b)   Sharing scripts will often bring people closer together than
if they have one each.
(c)   Allow time for discussion after scenes or acts.

(d) Give people the opportunity to change roles and not become typecast.

(e) If an individual seems to identify with a particular character or sentiment, develop this in improvisation if appropriate.

(f) Improvise new endings to plays the group know well.

(g) Give a traditional play a modern setting.

(h) Try developing the group's own ideas into play form — radio, television, theatre.

(i) Utilize tape recorder both for sound effects and recording completed work.

(j) Build plays around important group themes such as fear of anticipated treatment, leaving hospital.

THE DRAMA ROOM

1. As already stated only a space and some people are needed to "do" drama. You should obviously choose the most flexible room possible, but anywhere can be used. Try to have a space where everything does not have to be moved after each session. (But do not leave all equipment exposed or the lesson will start with a free-for-all.)

2. Experiment using colour not only in lighting but in decoration — have a black corner, sky-blue roof, angry-red grotto.

3. Have boxes, corners, fireplaces to provide hiding places.

4. Make use of any existing equipment, such as PE wall-bars, ropes and climbing-frames; mats, hoops, etc. — useful for stepping stones, magic places.

5. Have some area that can be drawn or painted on — floor, walls, blackboard.

6. Intermittent use of slide and film projectors, ultra-violet lighting valuable.

BASIC EQUIPMENT

The following are suggestions for basic equipment on a small budget. They are items that I have found particularly useful. Remember that many of these things, including lighting, can be borrowed from Educational and Hospital Supplies Departments. See also pages 12—13 on changing the environment and page 88 for details of art materials. Appendix III contains useful addresses for obtaining equipment, films and visual aids.

Record-player,
> stereo if possible, preferably manually operated to avoid
> waiting-time — mounting it on a shelf removes source of
> "temptation" and gives a firm base if the room vibrates.

Cassette tape-recorder and blank cassettes,
> model with "reporter's" microphone preferable.

Mains tape-recorder,
> for recording sessions (with group's knowledge) or for
> pre-recording music/sound effects (more useful for
> "finished" projects).

Adaptable rostra.

Suitable records.

Single spotlight plus colour filters; coloured lightbulbs.

Portable screens,
> for dividing up room, mounting visual aids.

Step-ladder.

Sturdy typewriter.

Posters obtainable from travel agents, British Rail, Dairy
> Council, trade organizations, Embassies, film companies,
> theatres.

Dressing-up box.

Art materials.

Musical instruments.

Polaroid camera and film.

Mask-making materials.

Junk box, for model building, experimenting.

Texture box, different things to feel, materials, sawdust, etc.

Treasure box, full of "beautiful things" (can be combined with
> texture box).

Large pieces sheeting, computer paper, string.

Unlimited newspaper.

12 Martyrs to Drama?

Having suggested the many ways in which drama can be developed in remedial work, I should not be surprised if some readers are feeling a little breathless! Before we all rush off and change class rooms into multi-media environments, I would like to give food for thought to the individual leader. From personal experience, I know how easy it is to become a "convert" to drama and to apply it to everything both on and off the timetable. Fine — if you can stand the pace!

However, remember that participatory teaching of this kind can be very demanding and tiring and I would suggest that those new to the medium try a little at a time.

To use drama seven or eight hours a day is a physical and emotional impossibility and the attempt can easily lead to creative overtiredness and disillusionment. This in turn will result in the drama itself becoming repetitive and boring.

However much we may believe in self-expression and the stimulation of oral skills, there are times when teachers and pupils need to be quiet. There are some school and hospital limitations that are impossible to overcome. There are days when willing voluntary helpers are away and when you, the leader, just don't feel in the mood. This is why I say, never become a martyr to drama!

Again, by becoming message-minded about creative work, we can lose the fun, that quality of healthy enjoyment which is so necessary to complement what is often a very dull, drab world. Always keep a sense of humour; if the group react light-heartedly to a serious topic — well why not? Nobody was more nonplussed than I, when a remedial group involved in a war project were practising a death scene — they shot me down with machine guns and as I was heaving around the room groaning before doing the "stage fall" one girl called out "Cor, Miss wants to go to the toilet!" We all collapsed in hysterics!

Be careful not to discharge all your own creative energy into your sessions or your group will be overwhelmed. Have your own outlets in a drama club or similar activities, and take the opportunities for stimulus provided by occasional workshops or learning new skills.

Try not to get to the point where you feel like one teacher who said to me "Drama's OK but it's such a drag." A good tonic to a failing sense of humour is to listen to Joyce Grenfell's nursery-school records. Drama is a taking as well as a giving situation, so if you feel it is too one-sided, have a rethink!

Remember that whatever the treatment, supportive or preventive work you may be doing, creativity is above all to be *enjoyed*.

APPENDIX I Training

During the past ten years there have been many associations and training organisations who are promoting short courses in remedial drama and dramatherapy. Readers should refer to the list of useful addresses in Appendix IV.

Those LEAs who have Drama Advisers will find many of them sympathetic to in-service courses in Remedial Drama. In recent years, Social Service Departments, Health Authorities, Probation Services, Playgroup Associations, University and College Departments have all been willing either to give grants to their employees or to mount courses themselves. However, for those who wish to complete a qualifying course in dramatherapy there are a number of courses that have been approved by the British Association for Dramatherapists.

It is the firm policy of the Association that courses should be post-professional/post-graduate and that students should not be accepted straight from college with no work experience. Students are expected to build on the firm foundation of their first qualification or degree, but also to have had experience in special education or psychiatry or in the community. Their dramatherapy training can thus be linked with their practical experience. Since all the courses that the Association has approved are part-time courses, students are expected to be in posts while they are following the course.

The colleges in question have all approached the Association to recommend an External Examiner so that the Association is able to keep some vigilance regarding the standards being accepted on the course in relation to both practical and written work.

The Association has a list of first qualifications which it will accept as being appropriate for dramatherapy training. It must be pointed out that a professional qualification with *no drama experience* is not acceptable, as dramatherapy courses cannot supply all the basics in terms of drama technique. Students without drama qualifications will either have had extended experience in university drama groups or have attended drama workshops as a developing interest.

The following range of first qualifications gives some idea but is not exhaustive:

> First qualification in: social work, occupational therapy, psychiatric nursing, special education, speech therapy, physiotherapy.

> First degree in: drama, psychology, medicine, anthropology, social science.

The following qualifying courses have been approved by the British Association for Dramatherapists:

> Two-year Dramatherapy Diploma (Hertfordshire College of Art and Design).

> Two-year Dramatherapy Course (Introductory and Advanced), College of Ripon and York, St John.

> Two-year course South Devon Technical College, Torquay.

N.B.   There are individual consultants who run courses in Dramatherapy and inquiries should be made to the Association, 7 Hatfield Road, St Albans, Herts, as to whether their courses are approved.

Useful Addresses

British Association for Dramatherapists, 7 Hatfield Road, St Albans, Herts.

British Association for Art Therapists, 13c Northwood Road, London, N.6.

Association of Dance Movement Therapy, 99 South Hill Park, London NW3 2SP.

Association for Professional Music Therapists, Music Therapy Unit, Harperbury Hospital, Harper Lane, Radlett, Herts.

Dramatherapy Consultants, 6 Nelsons Avenue, St Albans, Herts.

APPENDIX II Useful Reading in Drama, Remedial Drama and Dramatherapy

The following is a list of books and papers by the author, in chronological sequence of publication:

1973   *Remedial Drama* (Pitman, now A & C Black/Theatre Arts Books)

       'Ritual and its Links with Performance', paper presented at the Dramatherapy Conference, 1973

       'Ritual and Exploration', *Times Educational Supplement*, 7 December 1973

       'The Special Nursery: Explorations in Creative Play for Young Severely Handicapped Children', *Drama in Education 2*, ed. Hodgson and Banham (Pitman)

       'The Place of Drama in Education', *Self and Society*, vol. 1, no. 7

1975   'The Importance of the Body in Non-Verbal Methods of Therapy', *Creative Therapy*, ed. Jennings (Pitman)

1978   'Dramatherapy: the Anomalous Profession', *Dramatherapy*, vol. 1, no. 4

       'Beware of Drama', *Speech and Drama*, vol. 27, no. 3, ed. Ken Pickering (Society of Teachers of Speech and Drama)

       'Drama Therapy with the Institutionalised Disabled Adult', published by the Drama Advisers, County Durham

1979   'Drama and the Elderly', *Teaching Drama*, Winter/Spring 1979

       'Ritual and the Learning Process', *Dramatherapy*, vol. 2, no. 4

       'Theatre encounters therapy', *Therapy*, 18 January 1979

       Interview recorded in *Outlook*, journal of the National Association for Drama in Education and Children's Theatre, Autumn 1979

1981   'The Application of Dramatic Technique in the Learning of Social Skills', presented at UNESCO Conference, Paris, May 1981, and reprinted in *Dramatherapy*, vol. 5, no. 1

1981   'Dramatherapy with Multi-handicapped Children', *The Arts and Disabilities: a creative response to social handicap*, ed. Geoffrey Lord (Macdonald)

'Dramatherapy: history and origins', *Drama in Therapy*, ed. Courtney and Schattner (Drama Book Specialists, New York)

'Dramatherapy with Physically Handicapped People', *Drama in Therapy*, ed. Courtney and Schattner (Drama Book Specialists, New York)

'Drama and Learning with Mentally Handicapped People', paper presented at the Conference on the Creative Arts and Mentally Handicapped People, organised by the British Institute of Mental Handicap.

1982   'Dramatherapy and Social Identity', paper presented at the International Conference of Psychomotricity, Florence.

'The Importance of Anthropology for Therapists', GAPP/RAI, London.

1983   'From Theatre to Therapy' Kayley Memorial Lecture.

1984   'Dance, Anthropology and their contribution to Therapy', Dance Research Council, London.

Suggested Reading (a selective bibliography)

Allen, J., *Drama in Schools: Its Theory and Practice* (Heinemann, 1979)

Axline, V., *Dibs: in Search of Self* (Penguin, 1971)

Barker, C., *Theatre Games* (Eyre Methuen, 1977)

Berne, E., *Games People Play* (Penguin, 1964)

Blatner, H., *Acting In* (Springer, 1976)

Brandes, D. and Phillips, H. (eds), *Gamester's Handbook* (Hutchinson, 1979)

Brook, P., *The Empty Space* (Penguin, 1972)

Butler, L., *Games, Games* (Polytechnic of Central London, 1977)

Courtney, R., *Play, Drama and Thought* (Drama Book Specialists, New York, 1974)

Courtney, R., *The Drama Curriculum* (Heinemann, 1980)

Douglas, M., *Purity and Danger* (Penguin, 1970)

Goffman, E., *The Presentation of Self in Everyday Life* (Penguin, 1971)

Grotowski, J., *Towards a Poor Theatre* (Methuen, 1976)

Hanna, J., *To Dance is Human* (University of Texas, 1979)

Hodgson, J., *The Uses of Drama* (Eyre Methuen, 1977)

Hodgson J. & Richards, E., *Improvisation* (Methuen, 1979)

James, R. & Williams, P., *Guide to Improvisation* (Kemble Press, 1980)

Johnstone, K., *Impro* (Eyre Methuen, 1981)

Lewis, I., *Ecstatic Religion* (Penguin, 1971)

McGreggor, L. (ed), *Learning through Drama* (Schools Council and Heinemann, 1977)

Moreno, J. L., *Psychodrama*, 3 vols. (Beacon House, 1977)

Polhemus, T. (ed), *Social Aspects of the Human Body* (Penguin, 1978)

Priestly, P. & Maguire, J., *Social Skills and Personal Problem Solving* (Tavistock, 1978)

Robinson, K. (ed), *Exploring Theatre and Education* (Heinemann, 1980)

Scher, A. & Verall, C., *100+ Ideas for Drama* (Heinemann, 1975)

Slade, P., *Child Drama* (Hodder & Stoughton, 1976)

Slade, P., *Experience through Spontaneity* (Longman, 1968)

Slade, P., *Natural Dance* (Hodder & Stoughton, 1977)

Storr, A., *The Dynamics of Creation* (Penguin, 1976)

Turner, V., *Forest of Symbols* (Cornell, 1969)

Wagner, B. J., *Dorothy Heathcote: Drama as a Learning Medium* (Hutchinson, 1979)

Way, B., *Development through Drama* (Longman, 1967)

Wethered, A., *Drama and Movement in Therapy* (Macdonald & Evans, 1973)

Winnicott, D. W., *Playing and Reality* (Penguin, 1974)

Forthcoming

Drama Techniques in Clinical Practice (Winslow Press)

A Reader in Dramatherapy (Croom Helm)

Films

Veronica Sherborne, *In Touch*

Veronica Sherborne, *A Sense of Movement*

Veronica Sherborne, *A Question of Confidence*

Dorothy Heathcote, *3 Looms Waiting*

Dorothy Heathcote, *A Chance for Everyone*

These films are available from Concord Films, Ipswich, Suffolk

Sue Jennings, *Role Play with Maladjusted Adolescents* (Open University)

David Attenborough, *Spirit of Asia* (BBC television series)

'Malay Magic' (*Horizon*, BBC television series)

APPENDIX III The British Association for Dramatherapists

The British Association for Dramatherapists provides the following services:

* information, advice and support.
* a quarterly journal entitled *Dramatherapy*.
* links with other professional agencies in the creative therapies and arts.
* conferences and seminars.
* validation of training courses.
* recommendations on professional standards.

The Association has formed a Consultative Group with The British Association for Art Therapists and The Association for Professional Music Therapists in Great Britain to discuss areas of common concern.

The Association is negotiating with unions and employing authorities regarding pay and status of Dramatherapists and is working for greater recognition of Dramatherapy.

The Association is encouraging the formation of regional branches of the Association to provide conferences, skill sharing and support groups.

The Association is building up an archive of books, papers, articles, research etc. It will also publish occasional papers on specialised topics.

The Association has a large and divergent overseas membership and is encouraging communication and shared training events with other countries.

Membership

Full Membership. The usual requirement for entry is a post-professional dramatherapy qualification recognised by the B.A.D.Th. (Please note: full membership of the B.A.D.Th. does not automatically entitle members to practise in a psychotherapeutic setting. Such members are required to undertake additional approved psychodrama or group psychotherapy training.)

All full members are entitled to vote at the A.G.M., to be elected to the executive committee, to receive the quarterly journal *Dramatherapy*, and to reductions on certain training events.

Associate and Student Membership. This is open to all those who are interested in the aims of the Association or who are in training.

Associate and Student Members receive the quarterly journal and reductions on certain training events.

All enquiries to: B.A.D.Th. 7 Hatfield Road, St Albans, Herts.

Dramatherapy

This quarterly journal is the only publication of its kind, containing both theoretical articles and practical papers in this newly emergent field of dramatherapy. It has been in existence since 1977. You do not have to be a member of the Association to subscribe to the journal: many hospitals, libraries and other organisations do so. The address of *Dramatherapy* is 7 Hatfield Road, St Albans, Herts.

APPENDIX IV *Dramatherapy Consultants*

Dramatherapy Consultants has been established for many years and offers regular training, consultancy and therapeutic groupwork in St Albans and London, and more intermittently in the rest of Britai and Europe.

Consultation is available for Hospitals, Social Service Departments an Training Colleges for staff training and development, supervision as well as client referral.

Training through short courses and intensives is available both at an introductory and advanced level. Spring and Autumn Schools provi longer course in a variety of creative groupwork methods.

Supervision both for individual and group workers is provided on a regular basis in St Albans and London.

All information from the Director, Sue Jennings,

> Dramatherapy Consultants,
> 6 Nelsons Avenue, St Albans, Herts.
> Tel. St Albans 33069